CONSTITUTIONAL
CHAOS

CONSTITUTIONAL
CHAOS

WHAT HAPPENS WHEN THE GOVERNMENT
BREAKS ITS OWN LAWS

ANDREW P. NAPOLITANO

THOMAS NELSON
Since 1798

NASHVILLE   DALLAS   MEXICO CITY   RIO DE JANEIRO

Published in Nashville, Tennessee, by Thomas Nelson. Thomas Nelson is a registered trademark of Thomas Nelson, Inc.

Thomas Nelson, Inc. titles may be purchased in bulk for educational, business, fund-raising, or sales promotional use. For information, please e-mail SpecialMarkets@ThomasNelson.com.

Chapter Six is adapted from the author's comprehensive analysis of First Amendment juris-prudence, "Whatever Happened to Freedom of Speech? A Defense of 'State Interest of the Highest Order' As a Unifying Standard for Erratic First Amendment Jurisprudence," 29 Seton Hall Law Review 1197 (1999), which is available in its entirety at http://law.shu.edu/journals/ lawreview/library/29_4/nap.pdf, or from Westaw and Lexis/Nexis.

ISBN 978-1-5955-5040-8 (TP)

Library of Congress Cataloging-in-Publication Data

Napolitano, Andrew P.
    Constitutional chaos : what happens when the government breaks its own laws / Andrew P. Napolitano.
        p. cm.
    Includes index.
    ISBN 978-0-7852-6083-7 (HC)
    1. Justice, Administration of—Corrupt practices—United States—History. 2. Criminal justice, Administration of—Corrupt practices—United States. 3. Police corruption—United States. 4. Judicial power—United States. 5. Constitutional law—United States—Moral and ethical aspects. 6. Civil rights—United States. 7. War on Terrorism, 2001—Moral and ethical aspects. I. Title.
    HV9950.N365 2004
    345.73'052—dc22

                                                                            2004020596

Printed in the United States of America

10 11 12 13 14 RRD 21 20 19 18 17

Dedicated to

THOMAS MORE

Lawyer, Judge, Scholar, Chancellor of the Realm, Martyr, Saint.
Murdered by the Government
Because he would not speak the words
That the King commanded.

The nine most terrifying words in the English language are: "I'm from the government and I'm here to help."

—PRESIDENT RONALD REAGAN

Lady Alice More: *Arrest him!*

St. Thomas More: *For what?*

Lady Alice More: *He's dangerous!*

William Roper: *For all we know he's a spy!*

Margaret More: *Father, that man's bad!*

St. Thomas More: *There's no law against that.*

William Roper: *There is—God's law!*

St. Thomas More: *Then let God arrest him.*

Lady Alice More: *While you talk he's gone!*

St. Thomas More: *And go he should, if he were the Devil himself, until he broke the law.*

William Roper: *So, now you give the Devil the benefit of law!*

St. Thomas More: *Yes! What would you do? Cut a great road through the law to get after the Devil?*

William Roper: *Yes, I'd cut down every law in England to do that!*

St. Thomas More: *Oh? And when the last law was down, and the Devil turned round on you, where would you hide, Roper, the laws all being flat? This country is planted thick with laws, from coast to coast, Man's laws, not God's! And if you cut them down—and you're just the man to do it!—do you really think you could stand upright in the winds that would blow then? Yes, I'd give the Devil benefit of law, for my own safety's sake!*

ROBERT BOLT,
A Man for All Seasons

CONTENTS

CONTENTS

PART 4:
PROSPECTS FOR LIBERTY

INTRODUCTION
BREAKING THE LAW

It should be against the law to break the law. Unfortunately, it is not. In early twenty-first century America, a long-standing dirty little secret still exists among public officials, politicians, judges, prosecutors, and police. The government—federal, state, and local—is not bound to obey its own laws. I know this sounds crazy, but the events recounted in this book prove it true. *Constitutional Chaos* should be a wake-up call for every American who prizes personal liberty in a free society.

FRIEND NO MORE

Because it breaks the law, the *government* is not your friend.

When I arrived on the bench, I had impeccable conservative Republican law-and-order credentials. When I left eight years later, I was a born-again individualist, after witnessing first-hand how the criminal justice system works to subvert and shred the Constitution. You think you've got rights that are *guaranteed*? Well, think again.

Because the government breaks the law and denies it, the government is *not* your friend.

Eternal vigilance is the price of liberty, particularly when it comes to the American criminal justice system. Nowhere else does the state have greater raw power over an individual's life, liberty, and property. And nowhere else are our constitutionally guaranteed rights and freedoms under such a relentless, subtle, and ultimately devastating attack.

Because the government breaks the law and hides it, the government is not your *friend.*

The deck is grossly stacked in the government's favor. No wonder, as a recent *New York* magazine cover story put it, referring to the government's long winning streaks in criminal trials, "The Defense Rests—Permanently." No wonder that in 2003, fewer than 3 percent of federal indictments were tried; virtually all the rest of those charged pled guilty.

I know that you, like me, are concerned about what it means to be an American. Well, one thing I can tell you is that being an American means having certain rights, liberties, and personal freedoms *guaranteed* by the Constitution and the Bill of Rights. That's what it has always meant, and that's what it will continue to mean in these troubled times before us.

Most of us take these guaranteed rights and liberties for granted. Most of us live comfortable lives that never bring us into conflict with the criminal justice system. But in many ways, that's a *bad* thing, for if you had seen that system as I did, you would never take your guaranteed rights for granted again.

I am not fighting phantoms of lost liberties. I am talking about the things that the government does every day.

For example, even though the Constitution, through the First Amendment and Fourteenth Amendment, commands that neither the federal government nor the state governments can abridge the freedom of speech, you will see shortly that the government regularly prosecutes Americans for speaking freely and punishes them when they say things that the government doesn't want to hear. Despite the government's duty to use its power to protect us, you will see how the federal and state governments have failed to protect us and have enacted laws which make it impossible for us to protect ourselves. Despite the government's obligation to protect us from crime, you will learn that the government actually creates crime by setting traps for the ignorant, the naïve, the criminally inclined, and those it hates. Despite the protections from governmental abuse in the Fifth and Fourteenth Amendments, you will learn that the government literally breaks the law in order to enforce it, that it prosecutes people it knows to be innocent, that it seizes property from unwilling citizens and pays bargain basement prices for it only to flip that property to developers who earn a fortune on it. Despite the Constitution's promise of a presumption of innocence and a full and fair trial, in one of the more scandalous excesses of law enforcement, I have examined the government's behavior in bribing its own witnesses. If this bribery were done by defense counsel, it would no doubt result in the lawyer and the witness serving long jail terms.

The creation of the American republic with a written and popularly accepted Constitution, which shows a clear primacy for the individual over the government, is the greatest political achievement in the history of the Western world. The government's fidelity to the Constitution, which limits its powers and guarantees human liberty, is nowhere else more sorely tested than in wartime. Thus, we will examine if the government has been faithful to its obligation to guarantee rights and liberties since September 11th 2001. *It has not.* It has tortured people it has arrested. It has claimed the power to lock up Americans *for life* and not even bring charges against them. It has prosecuted foreigners in secret, arrested lawyers who presume to defend them, and for the first time in American history, without obtaining a court order, it reads Americans' mail and uses what it finds against them.

This is not the American government the Founding Fathers created.

NATURAL LAW AND THE SOURCE OF FREEDOM

For thousands of years philosophers, scholars, judges, lawyers, and ordinary folks have debated and argued over different theories suggesting the sources of human freedom. Though there are many schools of thought addressing these origins, most contemporary legal scholars in the Western world stand behind two principal theories about the origins of freedom: One school, the Natural Law theorists, argues that freedom comes by virtue of being human—from our own nature. The other school, the positivists, argues that freedom comes from the government.

Natural Law theory teaches that the law extends from human nature, which is created by God. Thus, the Natural Law theory states that because all human beings desire freedom from artificial restraint and because all human beings yearn to be free, our freedoms stem from our nature—from our very humanity—and ultimately from God. St. Thomas Aquinas, the principal modern interpreter of Natural Law, directly contends that because God is perfectly free and humans are created in His image and likeness, our freedoms come from God. The founders held this same basic view.

Such an understanding, that freedom comes not from government but from God, has profound effects on modern jurisprudence. It means, for example, that our basic freedoms, such as freedom of speech, freedom of the press, freedom of religion, freedom of association, freedom to travel, and freedom from arbitrary restraints, cannot be taken away by the government unless we are convicted of violating Natural Law—and the government can only convict us if it follows procedural due process.

Procedural due process means that we know in advance of the violations of Natural Law that the government will prosecute, that we are fully notified by the government of the charges against us, that we have a fair trial with counsel before a truly neutral judge and truly neutral jury, that we can confront and challenge the government's evidence against us, that we can summon persons and evidence in our own behalf, that the government must prove our misdeeds beyond a reasonable doubt, and that we have the right to appeal the outcome of that trial to another neutral judge or judges. This is the only way under Natural Law theory that any of our natural rights can be taken away.

Because free speech is a natural right and can only be taken away after due process, it cannot be legislatively taken away. Thus, Natural Law protects minority rights from incursion by the majority. Under Natural Law, neither Congress nor any state legislatures can declare that freedom of speech no longer exists. Since Natural Law posits that freedom of speech comes ultimately from God, the majority cannot legislate it away.

Natural Law also posits the existence of an independent judiciary with the power to stop a legislature and an executive from interfering with natural rights. Thus, under the Natural Law, if the Congress, for example, made it unlawful to speak out against abortion, or if a state governor stopped Christians and Jews from worshiping, judges can invalidate those acts, even if there were no First Amendment protecting freedom of speech and religion. Because the right to speak and worship as we wish comes from our humanity, not from the government or from the First Amendment, under Natural Law, judges can enforce those rights, notwithstanding the legislature or the executive.

Natural Law would also, of course, prevent the majority from having its way all of the time. For example, a legislature could not by majority vote take property that properly belongs to Person A and give that property to Person B. Why? Because under Natural Law, that legislation would exceed the power of any government by violating the right of Person A to the use and enjoyment of his own property. In fact, the Supreme Court of the United States, back in 1798, addressed just this situation.

The Connecticut Legislature enacted a statute taking property from one citizen and giving it to another. The highest court of the state of Connecticut invalidated the Legislature's act. The U.S. Supreme Court followed and upheld the Connecticut court and, in so doing, ruled that courts have the power to prevent legislatures from intruding upon natural rights because an act of any legislature contrary to the Natural Law cannot be considered a rightful exercise of legislative power. Thus, the court held, there are immutable natural rights that all human beings have that cannot be interfered with by a popular vote or the will of the legislature, but only through due process.

Under Natural Law, legislatures have unwritten limitations imposed upon them, and those limits prevent a legislature, no matter how one-sided the vote and no matter how popular the legislation, from enacting a law which interferes with a natural right. Theoretically, Natural Law proponents would argue that when the people created state legislatures and when the states created the Congress they never gave these legislative bodies the authority to interfere with natural rights.

Critics of Natural Law argue that it is anti-democratic because it prevents the majority from achieving its purpose. Moreover, they contend, since the Natural Law is not written down anywhere in precise legal language, it is impossible to tell what rights are protected by it and what are not. Thus, these critics conclude, a Natural Law theory of government reposes too much power in the hands of judges to decide what rights are natural and what rights are not, and what areas of human behavior may not be regulated or interfered with by the majority, either directly through a popular vote or indirectly through a legislative enactment.

Natural Law also commands certain prohibitions. For example, since taking an innocent life is always wrong, Natural Law commands that murder is unlawful, whether the legislature declares it so or not. Natural Law does, however, recognize that not all rights are natural and some do come from the state. For example, the right to drive a motor vehicle on a government-owned roadway is a right that comes from the state; hence, the government can lawfully regulate it (e.g., requiring a driver's license, limiting speed, etc.) and lawfully take it away (e.g., from habitual drunk drivers).

GOVERNMENT AS GIVER OF RIGHTS

Positivism is more or less the opposite of the Natural Law. Under Positivism, the law is whatever the government in power says it is. Positivism requires that all laws be written down, and that there are no theoretical or artificial restraints on the ability of a popularly elected government to enact whatever laws it wishes. *Carte blanche* all the way.

The advantage of Positivism is that, quite literally, the majority always rules and always gets its way, since there are no minority rights to be protected. Thus, to follow our earlier example, if, under a Positivism theory, a state legislature or the Congress were to enact legislation prohibiting public criticism of abortion, or a state governor were to prevent Christians and Jews from worshiping, so long as the legislature was legally elected and so long as the legislature followed its own rules in enacting the legislation and so long as the legislation proscribed criticism of abortion and authorized the governor's behavior, the prohibition on speech and the interference with the free exercise of religion would be the law of the land, and no court could interfere with it. If rights come from government, they can be repealed by government.

Critics of Positivism have argued that it leads to the tyranny of the majority. These critics remind us that Hitler and his Nazi government were popularly elected, and once in power, under the theory of Positivism, passed all sorts of horrific laws, all of which were *lawfully* enacted. Because there was no Natural Law to protect the minority, these awful laws became the law of the land.

In America, the Declaration of Independence is traditionally referred to as the anchor of our liberties. It is clearly a Natural Law document since in it Thomas Jefferson argues that our rights to life, liberty, and the pursuit of happiness come not from the government, but from our Creator.

The Constitution of the United States, as well, does not grant rights but rather recognizes their existence, guarantees their exercise, and requires the government to protect them. For example, the First Amendment to the Constitution reads in part, "Congress shall make no law respecting an establishment of religion or prohibiting the free exercise thereof; or abridging the freedom of speech. . . ." This clearly implies that the founders recognized that freedom of religious worship and freedom of speech come from some source other than the Constitution. The First Amendment, thus, is not a grant of rights to the people, but a restriction on government, preventing it from infringing on the rights the people already have. It also implies that not only may Congress not interfere with freedom of speech or the free exercise of religion, but Congress must prevent all who act in the name of the government from interfering with them as well.

This debate between the Natural Law and Positivism is more than academic and is quite relevant today.

Even though marriage is not discussed in this book, it crystallizes the two schools of legal thought. If the right to marry whomever you love is a natural right, then the government cannot regulate it. If the right to marry whomever you love comes from the state, then the government can regulate it.

WHAT'S AT STAKE IN AMERICA TODAY

Throughout this book we will be discussing rights and liberties. I understand rights to be specific freedoms specifically guaranteed by the Constitution, such as freedom of speech, freedom of the press, and the right to bear arms. I understand liberties to be more general freedom of actions with which the government may not interfere without due process.

I, myself, am a strong and fervent believer in Natural Law. The only valid laws are those grounded in a pursuit of goodness. Anything else—like taking property from Person A and giving it to Person B, like silencing an unpopular minority, like interfering with freedom of worship—is an unjust law, and, theoretically, need not be obeyed. St. Thomas Aquinas said only just laws impose an obligation of obedience, because unjust laws are not within the power of the government to enact; and only laws that seek goodness are just. This is the essence of Natural Law. No government may enact laws interfering with our freedoms no matter how popular the enactment.

The positivist would say since the government gives freedom, the government can take it away. The Natural Law says only God gives freedom and the government can only take it away as a punishment for violating the Natural Law, and then only through due process.

To a positivist, the government's goal is to bring about the greatest benefit to the greatest number of people. Under the Natural Law, the only legitimate goal of government is to secure liberty, which is the freedom to obey one's own free will and conscience, rather than the free wills or consciences of others.

The problem today in America—the greatest and gravest threat to personal freedom in this country—is that the positivists are carrying the day. Under their sway, the government violates the law while busily passing more legislation to abridge our liberties.

If we wish to survive the near future with our rights intact, we need to understand the size and scope of the threat. We must also understand its true identity: a government that breaks its own laws.

PART 1

RIGHTS AND LIBERTIES

1

BREAKING THE LAW TO ENFORCE IT

Amazingly, infuriatingly, incredibly, the government will lie, cheat, and steal in order to enforce its own laws. And the courts continually give law enforcement a free pass to engage in these practices.

The landmark 1952 U.S. Supreme Court case of *Frisbie v. Collins* established the principle that a court has the power to put a defendant on trial, even if law enforcement broke the law in bringing the defendant into the court's jurisdiction. It sounds inconceivable, but the Supreme Court has authorized the police to break the law, including abduction and kidnapping, in order to enforce the law.

ILLEGAL ABDUCTION

On February 19, 1942, police officers in Michigan asked their colleagues in Chicago to arrest one Shirley Collins. Chicago police officers met Collins at a bus station in Chicago, where they arrested and handcuffed him.

Complying with the request of the Michigan police, the Chicago police forcefully took Collins and held him in their custody. When he refused to answer questions until he could consult a lawyer, the Chicago cops and their Michigan colleagues, who had by now joined them, attacked Collins and beat him with blackjacks. Additionally, the Michigan police officers told the Illinois authorities not to let Collins consult with a lawyer or anyone else.

The next day, Collins requested a lawyer and was once again attacked by police officers until he was beaten into unconsciousness. The following day, the Chicago Police Department handed Collins over to the Michigan police officers, who carried him to Flint, Michigan, to face trial.

There is no question about the fact that the Michigan police kidnapped and abducted Collins. The entire sequence of events demonstrates that those law enforcement officers had utter contempt for the law they swore to uphold. Neither Illinois nor Michigan had a warrant for Collins's arrest. The Michigan police never made a request upon the Governor of Illinois for Collins's apprehension as a fugitive and for his extradition to authorities in Michigan.

Kidnapping is a federal crime, and the Anti-Kidnapping Act makes it illegal when an individual is "unlawfully seized, confined . . . kidnapped, abducted or carried away by any means whatsoever" across interstate lines. The federal kidnapping crime applies to both ordinary citizens and officers of the law: *No exception* is made in the statute for either state or federal law enforcement officers.

Accordingly, the Illinois and Michigan police committed a federal crime—kidnapping and abducting Collins from Illinois to Michigan—for the sole purpose of securing his presence in a courtroom in the state of Michigan.

Amazingly, the Supreme Court found absolutely no problem with this, adhering to the principle of *male captus, bene detentus.* That principle—translated as "badly captured, well detained"—permits the government to bring any defendant to trial regardless of whether he was improperly seized. According to the court, the government fully adhered to the Constitution's due process requirement by convicting Collins after a fair trial.

In the words of the Court of Appeals for the Sixth Circuit, the "practical effect" of the court allowing the kidnapping and abduction of Collins was "encouragement to the commission of criminal acts by those sworn to enforce the law." Essentially, the police are authorized to take any illegal step to bring a defendant into the courtroom. But due process doesn't start with a fair trial; the government's obligation to provide due process is triggered when police first make contact with a person.

The Supreme Court misconstrued due process, stating that there is no constitutional requirement that a court "permit a guilty person rightfully convicted to escape justice because he was brought to trial against his will." Being "brought to trial illegally" is different than being "brought to trial against his will." (Obviously, Collins was brought to trial against his will. What defendant would freely choose to go on trial for murder?) The Supreme Court ignored the exact purpose of federal laws prohibiting kidnapping and the constitutional right not to be confined unlawfully. If illegally abducting and kidnapping Collins doesn't constitute illegal imprisonment, what does?

The Supreme Court improperly allowed the police to put themselves above the law. When law enforcement uses force and violence illegally to bring a defendant into the courtroom, it is the court's duty to hold the police accountable for violating the defendant's constitutional rights.

In the criminal justice system, sometimes a "guilty" defendant walks free because the police illegally violated his constitutional rights. While this is unfortunate, the entire system would fall apart if courts failed in their responsibility to ensure that law enforcement does not place itself above the law. The police need a disincentive to keep them from breaking one law in order to enforce another. Regardless of whether Collins received a fair trial, his presence inside the Michigan courtroom was a result of the Illinois and Michigan police committing federal crimes.

FOREIGN FOLLIES

There is no limit to how far law enforcement will go in disregarding the law to promote the goal of apprehending criminals. Typical law enforcement behavior goes well beyond illegally abducting and kidnapping an individual so that he can be brought from Illinois to Michigan. The federal government has given itself the power, and the Supreme Court has not questioned that power, to invade the territorial integrity of a sovereign nation in order to abduct another country's citizen.

Humberto Alvarez-Machain is a physician, and a citizen and resident of Mexico. The United States Drug Enforcement Administration (DEA) had Machain indicted for his alleged participation in the murder and kidnapping of a DEA special agent. Subsequently, the DEA negotiated with a paid informant—an admitted former advisor to a Mexican drug lord—to abduct Machain and bring him to the U.S.

On April 2, 1990, six armed men broke into Machain's medical office, where they punched him in the stomach, shocked him with an electrical apparatus, and injected him with a substance that made him light-headed and dizzy. The men proceeded to fly Machain from Guadalajara, Mexico, to El Paso, Texas, by private plane. Upon arrival, Machain was handed over to the DEA and placed under arrest.

Mexico and the U.S. are each independent and sovereign nations. The two nations signed an Extradition Treaty in 1978 to recognize each other's territorial integrity and to prevent this exact sort of situation. The Mexican government formally protested the United States' kidnapping of Machain and promised to fully prosecute and punish him if he were returned.

The federal government has a constitutional responsibility to uphold treaties that the United States has entered into. The DEA clearly abused its power by refusing to arrange to extradite Machain in accordance with the Extradition Treaty, while making a secret deal with a paid informant to illegally and forcefully abduct Machain. Moreover, the forceful abduction of Machain is not only a violation of the treaty, but also a violation of international law. The United Nations Charter expressly prohibits this exact sort of international forceful abduction, respecting the territorial rights of all sovereign nations.

Machain challenged the government's assertion that U.S. courts have jurisdiction over a defendant who had been brought to the U.S. via an illegal, forceful abduction. A federal district judge in California and the U.S. Court of Appeals for the Ninth Circuit both agreed that the federal courts had no power to try Machain and ordered Machain's repatriation to Mexico. Yet, in a six-to-three decision in *United States v. Alvarez-Machain,* the Supreme Court ignored the obvious facts and law surrounding Machain's abduction and chose to affirm the principle that law enforcement has unlimited power to take illegal actions to bring a defendant into the jurisdiction and the courtroom.

The Supreme Court's majority concluded that the U.S.-Mexico Extradition Treaty did not expressly prohibit the U.S. government from paying an agent in Mexico to illegally and forcefully abuse, abduct, and kidnap a Mexican citizen who allegedly committed a crime in Mexico. This perverted interpretation of the treaty is utter nonsense; the U.S. is not free to take any action against Machain that the treaty does not expressly prohibit. As Justice Stevens wrote in dissent, the treaty also doesn't expressly prohibit the U.S. from torturing or executing Machain because it is more expedient or efficient than extradition, but that behavior would be unquestionably illegal.

Chief Justice Rehnquist wrote for the court that "whether [Machain] should be returned to Mexico . . . is a matter for the Executive Branch." Not so. It is the Supreme Court's job to stop the government when it breaks the law. Justice Stevens' dissent warned against the Court allowing the government to get away with breaking the law due to the "desire for revenge" against Machain's alleged contribution to a DEA agent's murder in Mexico.

Thus, the Supreme Court once again gave law enforcement officers a free pass blatantly to disregard the law—committing an illegal international abduction in a sovereign nation—in order to promote their interest in bringing a potential criminal to justice. When the government does this, due process is treated as a myth, and the courts turn a blind eye to the fact that the government breaks the law while trying to enforce the law. To the Supreme Court, all is dandy once the defendant arrives in the courtroom for his trial.

UNIVERSAL JURISDICTION

When the federal government breaks the law to bring a suspected criminal into the United States, the nation where the apprehension was made does not always protest as Mexico did with the abduction of Machain. In some situations, the federal government uses the threat of diplomatic might so that little attention is drawn to the illegal capture of the suspect.

Ramzi Ahmed Yousef, the mastermind of the February 1993 bombing of the World Trade Center in New York City, had eluded American law enforcement's capture for two years. On February 6, 1995, the FBI received information from an informant that Yousef would be arriving in Islamabad, Pakistan. The DEA and the State Department's Bureau of Diplomatic Security proceeded to raid Yousef's hotel room and brought him into the custody of the local Pakistani police. Without any legal proceeding or process, the Pakistani government secretly and informally surrendered custody of Yousef to the FBI. Yousef was then flown back to New York for trial.

The federal government, in removing Yousef from Pakistan without formal extradition proceedings, undoubtedly violated international and U.S. law. The government had significant leverage to manipulate Pakistan into illegally handing Yousef over in secret, because public extradition proceedings would have been a disaster with the Pakistani government trying to remain on good terms with Islamic extremists within its borders. And the Pakistani government—which is dependent on the U.S. for its security—wouldn't dare stand in the way of the U.S. government's illegal apprehension of Yousef.

The courts, once again, refused to impinge on the federal government's power and invented an absurd rationale for upholding the legality of Yousef's apprehension. Defying logic, Judge Kevin Thomas Duffy, a federal district judge in New York, ruled that Yousef was "'found' within the United States"! Since when is Islamabad, Pakistan, considered within the United States?

According to Judge Duffy, expounding on the concept of "universal jurisdiction," the whole world is considered to be within the United States! The Court of Appeals for the Second Circuit affirmed this absurd ruling, and the Supreme Court declined to hear the case.

Law enforcement and the courts must obey the law when they enforce the law, and even the most dangerous criminals are entitled to due process under the Constitution. A simple extradition request would have brought Yousef here legally and avoided the embarrassment and illogic of a judicial ruling standing for the principle that the "whole world is the United States."

LYING FOR A LIVING

Not only does the Supreme Court turn a blind eye when the government illegally kidnaps and abducts an individual to bring him into the courtroom, but the court has also repeatedly endorsed law enforcement's power to lie, cheat, and coerce when gathering evidence of crimes.

The Supreme Court upheld the police's power to lie, deceive, misrepresent, and coerce in the 1969 case of *Frazier v. Cupp*. The police suspected Martin Frazier and his cousin Jerry Rawls of murder. Before taking Frazier into police headquarters for questioning, the police asked him a few routine questions, including where he was on the night in question. Frazier admitted to being with his cousin Rawls, but denied being with the victim or any third person. The police began vigorous questioning after incompletely advising Frazier of his constitutional rights.

After Frazier continued to deny being with anyone but Rawls, his interrogators began a coercive and deceptive lying campaign. The officer falsely stated that Rawls had been brought into the station and that he had confessed to the murder. To try to prompt Frazier to talk, the officer began a tactic of sympathetically suggesting that the victim's homosexual advances toward Frazier had provoked a fight with Frazier and Rawls, and police and prosecutors understand that. The interrogator's lie caused Frazier to begin telling his story, but eventually he told the officer, "I think I had better get a lawyer before I talk any more. I am going to get into more trouble than I am in now." The interrogator continued the questioning and completely dismissed Frazier's request for counsel and his right to silence, replying, "You can't be in any more trouble than you are in now." Eventually, a full confession was obtained and was used against Frazier to convict him of murder.

There are limits to what the police can do to obtain a conviction, and despite his guilt, Frazier's interrogator clearly crossed that line.

In 1892, the Supreme Court in a case called *Bram v. United States* established the rule that a confession "must not be extracted by any sort of threats or violence, nor obtained by any direct or implied promises, however slight, nor by the exertion of any improper influence." The police indisputably misrepresented the facts in falsely stating to Frazier that Rawls had confessed to the murder. Frazier was also lied to when the interrogator denied his right to counsel, as he was incorrectly told that confessing wouldn't get him into any more trouble than he was already in.

Because the police used illegal tactics to coerce Frazier into a confession, Frazier's statement cannot be considered voluntary. Since involuntary confessions are inadmissible, the jury should never have heard Frazier's confession.

Yet, the Supreme Court ruled that the statement *could* be used against Frazier. Justice Marshall, writing for the court, admitted, "the police misrepresented the statements that Rawls had made." Furthermore, Justice Marshall went as far as stating that the interrogator's lies and representations were "relevant"! So, why didn't the court throw out Frazier's confession? According to the court, the misrepresentations were "insufficient in our view" based on "the totality of the circumstances." Rather than looking at the facts and explaining their conclusions, the court went no further than such convoluted legalistic phraseology. The court never stated why the interrogator's lies were "insufficient" and what other "circumstances" were used to comprise the "totality."

Put simply, the Supreme Court sent a message to law enforcement officers around the country that it was acceptable to lie and misrepresent facts and evidence in order to coerce a suspect into making a confession.

Justice Marshall's opinion makes it clear that the Supreme Court will look the other way when the police do not conduct themselves properly. The court even dismissed Frazier's request for a lawyer, stating that the interrogator probably took the request "not as a request that the interrogation cease but merely as a passing comment." Did the court really believe that "I had better get a lawyer before I talk any more" was "merely . . . a passing comment"? Why can't the court abide by its constitutional duty and honestly concede that police deception went too far?

In 1977, in the case of *Oregon v. Mathiason*, the Supreme Court once again sanctioned police deception. The victim of a burglary told an Oregon police officer who was investigating a crime that man named Carl Mathiason might have been involved. The police officer tried to find Mathiason with no success and left his business card at Mathiason's apartment with a note asking him to call because "I'd like to discuss something with you." Mathiason returned the phone call, and the officer asked when it would be convenient to meet.

The officer and Mathiason agreed to meet at the patrol office two blocks from Mathiason's apartment. Upon arrival, they shook hands and entered the office, where they sat across from each other at a desk. Mathiason was told that he was not under arrest, but that he needed to answer some questions about a burglary. The officer then told a blatant falsehood, misrepresenting to Mathiason that the police believed that he was involved in the burglary because his fingerprints were found at the scene of the crime. Within a few minutes of the officer's lie, Mathiason confessed that he had taken the property.

The Supreme Court of Oregon ruled that Mathiason was tricked by the officer's deceptive tactics into confessing—equatable with an involuntary or coerced confession. Coupled with the fact that Mathiason wasn't even advised of his *Miranda* right to remain silent until *after* the questioning ended, Mathiason's confession was suppressed.

However, the U.S. Supreme Court, overruling the Oregon Supreme Court, handed another victory to rogue cops and reinstated Mathiason's confession. The Court relied on a ludicrous line of reasoning, claiming that Mathiason really wasn't "in custody" when the statement was made. Such a claim relies on a meaningless formality, as Mathiason clearly was in custody: he was interrogated in privacy and in unfamiliar circumstances, the investigation focused on him, the police used coercive tactics, and he was not free to leave.

The court also illogically ruled that the police are allowed to lie, cheat, misrepresent, and coerce as long as the suspect being interrogated is not "in custody."

No matter what the circumstances were when the officer spoke to Mathiason, the officer abused his authority in lying that Mathiason's fingerprints were found at the house where the burglary occurred. The police should not be allowed to trick a suspect into a confession, whether the suspect is handcuffed in the interrogation room ("in custody") or voluntarily sitting in the interrogator's office but not free to leave ("not in custody"). But, as was the case with Martin Frazier's confession, the Supreme Court will still allow deception, lies, and coercion whether the suspect meets the formality that he is "in custody" or not.

HOME INVASION

When the police aren't illegally coercing suspects into making confessions, they may be found inside an individual's home illegally gathering evidence of crimes. While the Fourth Amendment forbids the police from conducting unreasonable searches and seizures, the Supreme Court has found a way to circumvent that constitutional guarantee.

The FBI suspected Nicodemo Scarfo, the son of incarcerated Philadelphia mob boss "Little Nicky" Scarfo, of masterminding a loan sharking and gambling operation in New Jersey and raided his office in January 1999. The agents copied the contents of Scarfo's computer hard drive, but were not able to read a single file. Scarfo had installed an encryption program on the computer, called Pretty Good Privacy, which requires the user to input a password in order to access the computer's files. The FBI tried to decipher Scarfo's password and also tried to break the encryption, but had no success at gaining access to the computer data.

Having failed to access Scarfo's files using standard law enforcement techniques, the FBI's last hope was to break the law. If the FBI agents were able to obtain Scarfo's password, they could simply type it in and bypass the encryption software. Accordingly, they sought to install a "key logger"—a device that records every single keystroke made by the computer user—on Scarfo's computer. The FBI would then be able to "capture" Scarfo's password once Scarfo typed his password into the computer and the key logger recorded those keystrokes.

Agents approached a federal magistrate judge about their failure to obtain Scarfo's password and asked for "authority to search for and seize encryption-key-related pass phrases" and to "install and leave behind [technologies] which will monitor the inputted data entered on [Scarfo's] computer by recording the key related information as they [sic] are entered."

U.S. Magistrate Judge Donald Haneke concluded that it was now acceptable for the FBI to break the law because "normal investigative procedures to decrypt the codes and keys necessary to decipher the . . . encrypted computer file *have been tried and have failed*" (my emphasis). With complete disregard for Scarfo's privacy, Judge Haneke authorized the FBI to break into Scarfo's office *as many times as necessary* to deploy, maintain, and remove "recovery methods which will capture the necessary key-related information and encrypted files."

On May 10, 1999, the FBI sneaked into Scarfo's office and installed the key logger. The specific key logging mechanism used is unclear. Even though Scarfo was suspected of loan sharking, not terrorism, the government cited "national security" concerns and refused to disclose any information about the mechanism to Scarfo's attorneys. The FBI's key logger most likely resembled either a hardware device (physically attached to Scarfo's keyboard) or a software program (running in the background and quietly recording keystrokes). The agents captured Scarfo's password, obtained access to all of the encrypted data on his hard drive, and then arrested him for gambling and loan sharking.

Scarfo's lawyers moved to suppress all of the evidence that the FBI obtained from their client's computer hard drive. They argued that because the FBI obtained Scarfo's password by unconstitutionally breaking into Scarfo's computer, everything that the FBI obtained from the computer is "fruit of the poisonous tree" and cannot be used in court.

Clearly, the FBI violated Scarfo's Fourth Amendment rights by conducting an illegal—though judicially authorized—search and seizure of his computer. The FBI's key logging is primarily unconstitutional because it is a secret means for the FBI to monitor every single activity that Scarfo conducted on his computer. The device recorded not only Scarfo's password but *every single character* that Scarfo typed into the computer! The key logger gave the FBI blanket permission to violate Scarfo's privacy in every way imaginable; they read letters that Scarfo typed, his medical records, and all his personal communications.

In the colonial period, British troops would ransack homes to conduct a "general search" for anything they wished to find. In today's digital age, the FBI's installation of a key logger on Scarfo's computer parallels the tyranny of King George III. In drafting the Fourth Amendment, the Founding Fathers expressed their contempt for this sort of privacy invasion by providing that law enforcement must have a warrant "particularly describing" what exactly is to be searched.

The FBI also failed to comply with the federal wiretap law, which requires the government to "minimize" the amount of information it records so that it only seizes specified information. Rather than dispute this notion, the FBI incredibly contended that the key logger was not a wiretap. Since a wiretap requires that communication be intercepted, the FBI insisted that it did not intercept any of Scarfo's communications. Whether the FBI actually intercepted communications is moot because recording the text of an email moments before the user hits the "send" button is equivalent to intercepting that email after it has been transmitted. And, the government refused to divulge to Scarfo's attorneys and *to the federal judge* how the key logger operated, effectively preventing Scarfo from demonstrating that the key logger was indeed a wiretap. Even though key loggers can be purchased for as little as fifteen dollars, the government amazingly asserted that the key logger was "a highly sensitive law enforcement search and seizure technique, the disclosure of which would compromise use of this technology . . . and jeopardize the safety of law enforcement personnel."

The federal district judge oversaw a series of procedural posturing between the government and Scarfo's defense team and was inclined to defer to the FBI's authority to install the key logger. The government, fearing that an appellate court was likely to order the FBI to disclose its key logging technology, and Scarfo sensing this fear, capitalized on an opportunity for minimal jail time, and thus he and the government negotiated a plea arrangement. On February 28, 2002, Scarfo pleaded guilty to a minor bookmaking charge that carried a two-to-three year prison sentence.

Unfortunately, privacy rights never got their day in court. Because appellate courts never had the opportunity to rule that the federal magistrate judge violated the Fourth Amendment by allowing the FBI to install the key logger on Scarfo's computer, there is no legal precedent to stop the FBI from continuing the practice. What is next? Does the FBI have the authority to put a key logger on the computer of every single American so that it can monitor every aspect of a person's private life?

The more courts allow the legal envelope to be pushed, the closer we inch toward that possibility.

POISONOUS TREE

In 1998 the Supreme Court heard the case of *Pennsylvania Board of Probation and Parole v. Scott*. Keith Scott's parole officer believed that Scott had violated a condition of his parole that he not own or possess any weapons. Parole officers arrested Scott, whereupon he surrendered his house keys. The parole officers drove to Scott's residence, where he lived with his parents, and awaited the arrival of Scott's mother. When she arrived, she refused to consent to a search, so they informed her that they were going to search Scott's bedroom without a warrant and without her consent. The parole officers found no evidence of a parole violation in Scott's room, and so they decided to search the rest of the house. In his mother's house they found five unloaded firearms—which were lawfully owned by Scott's stepfather and were unknown to Scott—and proceeded to recommit Scott to jail to serve three years of back time.

The parole officers conducted an illegal search: they entered Scott's mother's home without consent and without obtaining a warrant. In conducting this search, Scott's and his mother's Fourth Amendment rights were violated. According to the famous exclusionary rule of *Mapp v. Ohio*, the evidence gathered against Scott during the illegal search is considered "fruit of the poisonous tree" and cannot be used against him in court.

The Supreme Court decided that the Fourth Amendment didn't protect Scott, ruling that the exclusionary rule isn't a constitutional guarantee. Essentially, the court ruled that law enforcement may introduce illegally gathered evidence when the court says it can.

The five-to-four majority determined that the costs of applying the exclusionary rule exceeded the benefits, in terms of parole violations. Since when is the Supreme Court able to boil the Constitution down to a cost-benefit analysis? As Justice Souter noted in dissent, the Fourth Amendment becomes irrelevant if the police face no consequences, like the exclusion of the evidence they obtain, when they illegally gather evidence. This is yet another instance of the Supreme Court allowing law enforcement an unprecedented amount of power to violate the Constitution.

PLAYING DIRTY

In 1968, Andrew Muns and Edward LeBrun were shipmates aboard a U.S. Navy fueling vessel. Muns disappeared sometime during the night of January 17, 1968, but investigators couldn't solve the case.

As we've already seen, the federal government can get away with lying. So what's a little psychological manipulation and deception to coerce a suspect into confessing to a thirty-year-old murder?

In 1998, the Naval Criminal Investigative Services, Cold Case Homicide Unit reopened the case. The federal agents began to focus on LeBrun and interviewed him four times during late November 1999. When the investigators believed LeBrun to be the primary suspect, they brought him into a highway patrol station for a formal interview.

During their interview with LeBrun, the federal agents told one lie after another. Early in the interview, an agent told LeBrun, "There is absolutely no doubt that you are responsible for Ensign Muns' death. Absolutely no doubt about it. I know you know that. I know you believe it. I believe it." The agents then revealed a complete falsehood: they had two eyewitnesses to Muns' death and a suicide note written by a third individual who implicated LeBrun in Muns' death. LeBrun was also falsely told that the agents had "information and . . . evidence that is going to result in grand jury proceedings" and that he would be extradited to Alaska for a premeditated murder charge. The agents also threatened that they would ruin LeBrun's family's reputation and finances.

The federal agents went even further than these blatant lies. They had LeBrun speak to another agent masquerading as Muns's brother. The agents advised LeBrun that Muns's family was prepared to forgive him if he admitted to a spontaneous killing. Knowing that LeBrun himself was a cancer survivor, the agent posing as Muns's brother revealed that he also had cancer, had only a short time to live, and wanted to know everything about his "brother's" death. This caused LeBrun to get emotional and start spilling details of the crime.

As if all this law enforcement deception weren't enough, the federal agents even *promised* not to prosecute LeBrun if he confessed to spontaneous murder. LeBrun asked the agent, "So, am I hearing that I won't be prosecuted?" The agent replied, "That's what you are hearing." LeBrun asked once again, "Is that what I am hearing?" And the agent stated, "That's what you are hearing." A second agent added, "If it's spontaneous and that's the truth, you will not be prosecuted." The first agent followed up, "That's absolutely right."

Shortly thereafter, LeBrun confessed to murdering Muns and was prosecuted.

LeBrun's confession was a direct result of federal agents lying, cheating, misrepresenting evidence, coercing, deceiving, and making false promises.

Because it was involuntary, the confession cannot be used against him in court. The federal district judge ruled as such; so did a three-judge panel of the U.S. Court of Appeals for the Eighth Circuit. However, the full Court of Appeals, in *United States v. LeBrun*, reinstated LeBrun's confession despite the extreme steps of the federal agents.

Despite one hundred years of Supreme Court precedent stating that a confession may not be obtained via a false promise, the court found the promise to be only "one factor." It reasoned that, because LeBrun was intelligent, he perceived the promise as a loophole in the prosecution's case and tried to take advantage of it. When did federal courts get in the business of reading minds rather than following the law?

Recently, the New York Police Department tried to coerce an innocent man into confessing to the murder of his friend. On January 12, 2003,

Burke O'Brien was fatally shot in the chest while he and Forrest Bloede were attempting to return home from a night of clubbing.

Bloede told the investigators that two muggers took twelve bucks from O'Brien, and then shot O'Brien when he moved to regain possession of the money. Yet, the investigators did not believe Bloede and were determined to bring him down, even if they had to lie, coerce, cheat, and misrepresent. In order to elicit a confession, the investigators falsely told Bloede that O'Brien had survived the shooting. The ploy failed, and the police released Bloede after further forensic evidence and eyewitness statements substantiated Bloede's original account. It is an outrage that the police can actually get away such a blatant lie and can almost cause an innocent man to confess simply because he does not know what other illegal tactics the police have up their sleeves.

State and federal law enforcement officers continually lie and get away with it. These individuals have sworn to uphold the law, yet they place themselves above the law, and the courts do nothing to stop it.

GOOD FOR GOOSE, BAD FOR GANDER

Not only does the federal government break the law by lying, but it also prosecutes individuals for doing the exact same things its agents do!

Martha Stewart—private-citizen-turned-lifestyle-celebrity—was targeted by federal government officials trying to make names for themselves.

Stewart owned about four thousand shares of stock in ImClone Systems Inc., a pharmaceutical company developing a cancer drug. ImClone stock traded at seventy dollars in late 2001. But in December 2001, government bureaucrats at the Food and Drug Administration (FDA) leaked word that the FDA was preparing to reject ImClone's application seeking approval of its cancer drug. On December 28, the FDA publicly released this information, and ImClone shares lost 18 percent of their value on the following trading day.

The day before the public FDA announcement, December 27, Stewart sold all of her ImClone shares at about fifty-nine dollars per share. The FBI, the Securities and Exchange Commission, and the U.S. Attorney's Office in Manhattan interviewed Stewart on February 4, 2002. When the government accused her of selling the stock based on information that the price was going to fall, Stewart told investigators that she and her stockbroker had prearranged to sell the stock if the price fell below sixty dollars a share.

There was not a single thing illegal about Stewart's stock sale. The federal government didn't even accuse her of insider trading (she wasn't an insider) or fraud. Because the government wanted to attack a high-profile female target, it successfully convinced a jury that Stewart was guilty of "lying to investigators," "obstruction of justice," and "conspiracy." The best the government could claim was that Stewart made false statements, not perjury (which is a false statement under oath), to government officials during an interview.

Only Stewart knows whether the stock was sold based on prearranged instructions or because Stewart knew that the FDA had rejected ImClone's drug application. At worst, she simply told a lie to get the investigators off her back—a perfectly natural reaction.

Agents and employees of the federal government lie all the time and get away with it; Stewart can lie too, right?

Not hardly.

According to the federal criminal code, it is a crime to lie to federal officials. This law criminalizes *all lies* stated to the federal government, not just lies to federal investigators *investigating crimes*. It is anyone's guess why employees of the federal government can lie to private citizens without penalty, but private citizens can go to jail for lying to the federal government even when they are innocent.

Do FBI agents and local and state police have some moral superiority that permits them to lie in the course of their work and yet allows them to prosecute non-law enforcement citizens who lie in the course of their work? Does the Constitution give the federal government this kind of power? Why don't the laws apply to all of us?

THE BENCH STRIKES BACK

As a judge, I once presided over a preliminary hearing over a defendant's motion to suppress evidence he said was illegally seized.

Typically, at such a hearing, the defendant asserts that the police unlawfully seized evidence in violation of the Fourth Amendment, and the government must prove to the court that it seized the evidence legally. In such a hearing, the defendant need not prove anything.

This particular defendant was charged with possession of cocaine and possession of cocaine with the intent to distribute it. The government often attempts to prosecute individuals for possessing drugs with the intent to distribute them, even though that individual has *absolutely no intent* to distribute drugs. The basis of the government's concocted argument is that if an individual possesses more cocaine than a normal user could possibly use within that cocaine's shelf life, that individual *automatically* has an intent to distribute that cocaine. The government once again thinks it can read minds in order to prosecute individuals for a crime that it thinks an individual might commit.

So, the police stopped this defendant, a young man driving a large sedan through a known drug corridor (the New Jersey Turnpike) with out-of-state license plates. The police are notorious for stopping drivers who fit this profile, and their suspicions frequently prove to be correct. But since the police have no lawful basis for stopping a driver simply based on their hunch that the driver possesses drugs, they concocted a story that this defendant had a cracked taillight (a lawful basis for pulling the defendant over). The defendant asserted that the *police* cracked his taillight *after* they made the stop, to give the impression that they lawfully asked the defendant to pull over.

When the police officer who made the stop was on the witness stand,

I asked him where he was positioned when he spotted the defendant's allegedly broken taillight. I did a quick calculation in my head and realized that he was three-tenths of a mile away from the defendant's vehicle. I asked the officer if he *really* could see a crack in a taillight at three-tenths of a mile away, and he replied, "Yes, your honor!"

The officer proceeded to testify that he patted down the defendant after making the traffic stop. While a search must ordinarily conform to the Fourth Amendment's search and seizure requirements, meaning the police need a search warrant, a police officer may, without a warrant, conduct a pat down search for *weapons*. Since this pat down search is an exception to the Fourth Amendment designed to protect the police, the officers are not permitted to search for anything else but weapons.

Yet, this particular officer patted down the defendant and found a *bag of cocaine*. He testified that he felt a *brick* in the defendant's pocket, and that he was sure that the defendant had that brick to use as a weapon against him. I didn't believe the officer's claim that he could see a crack in a taillight at three-tenths of a mile, nor did I believe that a bag of cocaine could feel like a brick. So I asked the prosecutor if the bag was in the courtroom. It was, and I asked the clerk to bring me the bag.

"The court is going to squeeze the bag to see if it feels like a brick," I announced.

I squeezed the bag, and it broke!

Cocaine spewed all over me, including on my hair, face, eyebrows, and robe. As the courtroom audience sat in silent shock, I said, "Only in America can a black-robed judge sit in a public courtroom covered in cocaine, with impunity." My security team vacuumed up the cocaine, and I dismissed the case because the cop was not worthy of belief: *He lied under oath.*

I once heard an infuriating case involving the owner of a small Italian restaurant, himself an immigrant from Italy, who was visited by two well-dressed gentlemen who introduced themselves and asked for weekly payments of a hundred dollars. In return, they promised the restaurant owner that his garbage would be collected on time, that he would not have any trouble with labor unions, that he would not be the victim of any crime, and that no competing restaurant would open in his neighborhood.

He threw them out.

They returned unannounced about six times and every time their demands increased, eventually to a thousand dollars a week, each. After he rebuffed that demand, they said they'd be back the following week with guns, and so he'd better get one. Terrified of this threat, and afraid as most immigrants are to involve the police, the restaurant owner borrowed a friend's gun.

When the two gentlemen returned and asked if he had a gun, the restaurant owner reached into a drawer, pulled out the gun, and pointed it at them. They immediately slapped handcuffs on him! Unbeknownst to him, they were New Jersey state troopers who were either trying to shake him down for money or coerce him into breaking the law.

His prosecution for carrying a gun was assigned to me. The same two state troopers had also visited a nearby Italian bakery and, while consuming cannoli and espresso, asked the owner for a shot of sambuca in their espresso. When the owner complied, he, too, was put into handcuffs and arrested. The charge was selling liquor, *even though he gave it away*, without a license! This case was also assigned to me.

Before the case began, I ordered the troopers to appear in my courtroom, to inquire if their schemes were self-directed or authorized by their supervisors. They refused to be so interrogated, whereupon the *prosecutors* asked me to dismiss both cases, which I did. When I announced that the charges were dismissed, the bakery owner wailed in delight, and in a classic Sicilian accent proclaimed: "The Judga, he can eata for free for the resta his life!"

I never took the owner up on his offer of free meals for life, but I did appreciate his sentiments. Rarely do prosecutions based on police lies and entrapment end so happily for the unfortunately accused.

2

ATTACKING THE INNOCENT

Even in America, checks on government law breaking can be evaded. Just as a deranged Josef Stalin could put a random citizen into the Gulag and throw away the key, on occasion the law enforcement system in the United States is equally despicable.

PROTECTING THE GUILTY

As a result of moral corruption in law enforcement in Boston, from local police and prosecutors all the way up to the Director of the Federal Bureau of Investigation, an entirely innocent man spent thirty years of his life behind bars. Amazingly, the police and FBI arrested this man, and the prosecutors charged and prosecuted him to conviction, despite *knowing that he was innocent*.

Joseph Salvati's worst mistake was that he got involved with the wrong crowd. Salvati had borrowed four hundred dollars from a loan shark to satisfy a gambling debt, and the loan shark felt that Salvati was too slow in repaying the debt. The loan shark happened to be a friend of Joseph "The Animal" Barboza, a hit man for the Patriarca crime family, New England's most powerful Mafia group. According to a memo written by a Boston police sergeant, Salvati's failure to repay Barboza's friend "angered Barboza to retaliate by throwing [Salvati] into the mix."

Here's the background: On March 12, 1965, mob boss Ray Patriarca ordered a hit on a small-time hoodlum named Edward "Teddy" Deegan. Deegan had previously angered some members of the Boston mob by brandishing a gun in a restaurant. Accordingly, "Jimmy the Bear" Flemmi, a hit man, like Barboza, for the Patriarca family, arranged for Deegan to be murdered in a back alley in Chelsea, Massachusetts.

The FBI knew about the hit on Deegan two days *before* it happened. On March 10, 1965, an FBI informant told Special Agent H. Paul Rico that Patriarca had ordered Flemmi's murder of Deegan. Rico's report reads, "Informant advised that he had just heard from Jimmy Flemmi, and Flemmi told the informant that Raymond Patriarca has put out the word that Edward 'Teddy' Deegan is to be 'hit,' and that a dry run has already been made and that a close associate of Deegan's has agreed to set him up."

A memorandum written on March 19, 1965, one week after the murder, from the FBI Special Agent in Charge in Boston to FBI Director J. Edgar Hoover himself revealed that the Boston police and the FBI concluded that Flemmi was present at the murder scene and that his underling had fired the fatal shot into the back of Deegan's head. The FBI and the police clearly recognized Flemmi's motive for murdering Deegan and understood the Mafia politics involved, but chose not to prosecute Flemmi because he had been working as an FBI informant.

Several months later, Boston FBI agents sent another memo to J. Edgar Hoover informing him that Flemmi had killed Deegan but that it wasn't prudent to prosecute him. This June 9, 1965, memo noted that "from all indications, [Flemmi] is going to continue to commit murder" but "the informant's potential outweighs the risk involved." So the government let a murderer roam free because of his *potential.* In 2002, the U.S. House of Representatives Government Reform Committee concluded that J. Edgar Hoover himself had tacitly approved the decision not to prosecute Flemmi for the Deegan murder.

The case sat idle for a few years, until Joe Barboza found himself in jail in 1967 for a parole violation. The federal government's case against

Barboza was substantiated by the fact that the FBI informant—"Jimmy the Bear" Flemmi—was ready to turn his back on Barboza. So, Barboza decided to cooperate with the government and become the first ever member of the FBI's Witness Protection Program. Barboza agreed to testify against Patriarca and his underboss in key Mafia cases that the FBI hoped would help bring down the New England Mafia.

Once Barboza was cooperating with the government, FBI Special Agents Rico and Dennis Condon—knowing full well that Flemmi was responsible for the Deegan murder in 1965—demanded that Barboza testify against the Boston mob in that murder case and implicate "someone of importance." *It was time for Barboza to seek revenge against Joseph Salvati for his failure to repay the four hundred bucks.*

Barboza vowed never to allow his friend Flemmi "to fry" and worked with the FBI agents to manufacture a lie whereby he would implicate Salvati and five others in the Deegan murder. Since eyewitness reports noted that the actual triggerman was balding, and since Salvati at the time had a full head of hair, incredibly, the FBI agents convinced Barboza to maintain that Salvati was wearing a disguise as a bald man that evening.

Shortly thereafter, the Special Agent in Charge of the Boston FBI wrote to J. Edgar Hoover that Agents Rico and Condon had, "via imaginative direction and professional ingenuity," caused Barboza to turn against the New England Mafia. The agents received monetary bonuses and commendations from Hoover.

And in October 1967, the FBI made the final decision to ruin an innocent man's life. Joseph Salvati was indicted for the murder of Teddy Deegan, though the government knew he was innocent.

The prosecutors were determined to obtain a conviction at any cost. During the trial, the Boston prosecutors' case rested on nothing more than the words of Barboza, the government's sole witness. The prosecution buttressed its weak, concocted case by concealing exculpatory evidence from the defense, including a report from the Chelsea Police Department concluding that Deegan's killer was Flemmi, not Salvati.

Even thirty-five years later, James McDonough, who second-chaired the prosecution, would not admit that the government's behavior was itself criminal. In 2002, he testified before Congress that the exculpatory evidence which he withheld from Salvati's defense had "serious evidentiary problems" and was mostly hearsay. But he *knew* that it was true!

The FBI quietly watched as Boston prosecutors used Barboza to make the case against Salvati. Of course, the FBI did not turn over a shred of evidence to the prosecutors that would lead them to the real killer or would in any way implicate the FBI in orchestrating a sham case against Salvati. On July 31, 1968, Salvati was convicted of murder.

Since Barboza's testimony was skyrocketing the careers of Special Agents Rico and Condon, the agents decided to return the favor. In 1970, Barboza's parole was revoked based on a gun possession violation. During these proceedings, Barboza told his attorney, F. Lee Bailey, that he wished to "set the record straight as to certain perjured testimony he had given in state and federal courts" and admitted that he had had falsely stated that Salvati was responsible for the Deegan murder. Knowing that Barboza was afraid to return to the general prison population where he would be recognized as a government snitch, Special Agents Rico and Condon "coerced" Barboza into changing his mind about recanting his perjured testimony by arranging for Barboza's release from prison.

Several months later, Rico and Condon once again came to Barboza's rescue. In 1971, California prosecutors charged Barboza with first-degree murder, and the two FBI agents traveled to California and testified on his behalf. Barboza shot the victim twice in the *back of the head*, yet he invoked a claim of *self-defense*. Instead of receiving a life—or death—sentence, Barboza went to jail for four years.

On February 11, 1976, three months after his release, Barboza was gunned down on a San Francisco street. Barboza ate lunch with another FBI informant immediately before he was murdered, and the government took sixteen years to indict the shooter. Perhaps this is not merely coincidental, and the FBI felt that Barboza was a liability.

In May 2001, Special Agent Rico testified before Congress and refused to admit that he framed an innocent Salvati. Despite the plethora of evidence suggesting otherwise, including *Rico's own notes and memoranda*, Rico maintained that the FBI had no knowledge that Flemmi killed Deegan, and he maintained that it hid no evidence.

When Connecticut Congressman Christopher Shays noted that Rico felt absolutely no remorse for sending an innocent man to prison for thirty years, Rico shot back, "What do you want, tears?" Rico refused to take any responsibility for his actions, testifying that "I feel we have a justice system and how it plays out, it plays out." Shays responded, "You just don't give a f—, do you?"

Meanwhile, in the 1970s and 1980s, Joseph Salvati remained wrongly imprisoned without a soul to advocate for him, until attorney Victor Garo decided to take the case *pro bono*. In 1989, the Massachusetts Parole Board unanimously voted to commute Salvati's sentence, but the commutation never reached the desk of Governor Michael Dukakis for his approval.

When the commutation request finally reached Governor William Weld in 1993, he declined to commute Salvati's sentence. The reason was that high-ranking Massachusetts officials were opposed to Salvati's commutation; Special Agent Condon was by then the head of the Massachusetts Department of Public Health. But as the exculpatory evidence began to be revealed, Governor Weld had a change of heart and commuted Salvati's sentence in December 1996.

After thirty years in prison, Salvati saw freedom on March 20, 1997.

But the Boston prosecutors and the FBI weren't going to allow Salvati to breathe free air for too long. They reopened the case in order to bring a new change against him.

Finally, in January 2001, a judge exonerated Salvati, and the prosecutors agreed not to pursue the case further. At the request of the FBI, the federal government refused even to discuss a financial settlement with Salvati. While he has filed a three-hundred-million-dollar lawsuit against the federal government (how do you put a value on thirty years of *inten-*

tionally wrongful imprisonment?), the Federal Tort Claims Act makes it almost impossible for the government to be found liable.

This law was enacted to enable individuals to sue the federal government for negligence, but includes a "discretionary function" exception that bars virtually every lawsuit. The statute shields the government from liability when one of its agents performs a "discretionary function or duty . . . *whether or not the discretion involved be abused.*" The government only has to assert that since its FBI agents had discretion to frame Salvati, it is simply irrelevant that they blatantly abused their discretion! The fact that they should have no such discretion is apparently irrelevant.

It is unfathomable that the government could have been so morally corrupt at every stage in the process, from the Boston police to the FBI agents to the Boston prosecutors to the governor of Massachusetts and even to J. Edgar Hoover.

Salvati went from owing a mere four hundred dollars to a loan shark to being the victim of one of the most outrageous law enforcement scandals in the history of Massachusetts. Not one individual in the government blew the whistle in order to prevent an innocent man from serving thirty years of prison time. And FBI headquarters still bears J. Edgar Hoover's name. It is amazing that the truth of the FBI's framing of Salvati ever came to light. Think how many other unjustly incarcerated individuals are never so fortunate as to be exonerated.

JANET RENO'S MIAMI VISE

It doesn't only happen in Boston. As the state attorney for Dade County, Florida, Janet Reno made a name for herself by prosecuting innocent people so that they could rot in prison for crimes they did not commit.

In the 1980s, an increasing number of mothers entered the workforce, leading to a proliferation of daycare centers. Janet Reno, recognizing that parents had no way of confirming whether their children were safe at these daycare centers, took advantage of these societal fears. Reno accused numerous daycare operators of being child molesters, and created a national paranoia and frenzy so that the public would rally to her side.

Reno pioneered the "Miami Method" of prosecuting child sex abuse cases, by manipulating juries instead of presenting any physical evidence in order to convict these daycare operators. While ruining the lives of numerous innocent people, Reno gained national prominence that would leverage her to an appointment from President Bill Clinton to serve as attorney general of the United States.

Janet Reno found the perfect target to make national headlines and bolster her career. Grant Snowden, happily married with two children, was a decorated police officer who had been honored as South Miami's 1984 Police Officer of the Year. To earn some additional money for the family, Snowden's wife cared for several neighborhood preschool children. But in 1985, a three-year-old, for whom Snowden's wife cared, told his parents that Snowden had touched him sexually.

The police and prosecutors conducted an investigation and dropped the case because there was no evidence to substantiate this allegation. However, two months later, Reno reopened the investigation, and, in April 1985, Reno charged Snowden with having molested a three-year-old girl in 1977, eight years earlier.

The case against Snowden was amazingly pathetic: there was no physical evidence of abuse; the young girl had made similar allegations against another man several years earlier which turned out to be false; and the girl wasn't present at the Snowden house at the time of the alleged abuse, as demonstrated by cancelled checks suggesting that a different babysitter was caring for the girl at the time. A jury returned a not-guilty verdict in a matter of hours.

Reno couldn't accept the fact that she had failed twice to send this targeted innocent man to prison. David Markus, lead prosecutor, noted that his office "learned from the first case . . . that the jurors . . . didn't believe the *one* child." So, Reno ordered her office to build a gargantuan case against Snowden.

Reno found five new children to fabricate allegations of sexual abuse against Snowden. While none of the children was a credible witness, Reno's theory was that the jury would be duped into believing the children if it heard from all five of them in a single case. Thus, Reno's strategy—the "Miami Method"—was to overwhelm the jury with numerous bits of phony "evidence," so that the prosecutors could eventually convince the jurors that all of the "evidence" was true.

Reno recruited Laurie Braga to interview all five of the children who brought allegations of sexual abuse against Snowden. Reno portrayed Braga, who had no training as a psychologist but had a Ph.D. in speech, as a "child abuse expert." A Cornell psychology professor noted that Braga "underwent extremely suggestive interviews" with the children which made "the determination of accuracy [of the allegations] impossible."

Every single allegation that the children made against Snowden was first suggested to them by Braga, and Braga even hypnotized the children into "fantasy-land." These deplorable techniques are confirmed by a transcript of one of these interviews: The first thirty-three pages show Braga suggesting that different sorts of sexual activity happened to each child, and then Braga began to confuse pretense with reality when the child wasn't taking to her suggestions. By having the child pretend that Snowden did something wrong, the child began to believe that the sexual abuse happened so that Braga could merge the fantasy into real events.

Braga testified to the jury that children *never* lie and *can't* be brainwashed into believing something that is not true (did she forget about Santa Claus and the Tooth Fairy?). Snowden's attorneys were not allowed to refute the prosecution's experts and weren't permitted to tell the jury that he had just been acquitted in another case. Additionally, they were not allowed to challenge the "medical evidence" that the state presented. This "medical evidence" was completely manufactured; the jury heard that one of the children was "diagnosed" with Gardnerella vaginitis. A Rape Treatment Center physician noticed some moisture and redness on the girl, looked at it under a microscope, and proclaimed that the girl was infected. The physician immediately disposed of the evidence, without performing a medically accepted test that could have reliably confirmed the infection.

On March 7, 1986, the jury returned a guilty verdict on all five sexual battery counts. The judge sentenced Snowden to five life terms. All of Snowden's appeals were denied until the U.S. Court of Appeals for the Eleventh Circuit heard his *habeas corpus* petition in 1998. After Snowden had spent twelve years in prison, the Eleventh Circuit vacated his conviction and set him free. The court ruled that "allowing expert testimony [from Braga] to boost the credibility of the [children who were making the allegations] against Snowden—considering the lack of other evidence of guilt—violated his right to due process by making his criminal trial fundamentally unfair." Essentially, Braga scammed the children into making false allegations against Snowden and then unconstitutionally made up the jury's mind for them. An expert witness cannot tell the jury that *it must be true* that children do not lie; the jurors themselves must have been able to *decide* whether the children were telling the truth.

TORTURE AND PSYCHOLOGICAL ABUSE

The victims of Janet Reno's child molestation hysteria do not always have happy endings. Thanks to a fallacious case drummed up by Reno, Frank Fuster remains incarcerated for 165 years without the possibility of parole. Janet Reno began the notorious "Country Walk" case in 1984, as she faced a serious challenger in her bid for reelection as Dade County's state attorney.

In August 1984, Frank Fuster and his wife, Ileana Fuster, were arrested for sexually abusing more than twenty children who attended their home daycare center. Reno began the case by soliciting Laurie Braga and her husband Joe Braga, also a "child abuse expert" with no psychology training and with a doctorate in education, to interview the children.

The Bragas used the same suggestive and misleading interview techniques as those that were condemned and struck down by the Eleventh Circuit in the Snowden case to elicit false accusations from the children in this case. The children were brainwashed with fantasies of sexual abuse involving masks, snakes, drills, and other objects, and eventually came out of the interviews thinking that they were victims.

Of all the children alleging sexual abuse against Fuster, Reno's office only presented physical "evidence" that *one child* was abused. The prosecution invoked a laboratory test suggesting that a child had tested positive for gonorrhea of the throat. However, the lab test that was performed is very unreliable and often gives false positives. Reno's agents tested for the family of bacteria to which gonorrhea belongs rather than specifically for gonorrhea; other bacteria that could have caused the false positive are harmless and are frequently found to live in children. Of course, the state ordered the lab to destroy the evidence three days later, thereby preventing the defense from challenging the state's phony "evidence."

Recognizing that the case against Fuster was weak, Janet Reno's final straw was physically and mentally torturing Ileana Fuster to a point where Ileana could be coerced into implicating her husband.

Reno had Ileana isolated from the prison population and placed in solitary confinement, *naked.* Ileana described her treatment in a 1998 interview: "They would give me cold showers. Two people will hold me, run me under cold water, then throw me back in the cell naked with nothing, just a bare floor. And I used to be cold, real cold. I would have my periods and they would just wash me and throw me back into the cell."

The psychological torture began with prison officials taking Ileana out of jail at night and bringing her to restaurants in Miami. The officials would return her to solitary confinement and tell the seventeen-year-old, "If you ever want to see a restaurant like that again, you'll testify against Frank Fuster. Because you'll grow to be an old woman here in this prison." Janet Reno employed a series of psychologists and therapists to try to hypnotize and brainwash Ileana, to no avail.

Late one night, the naked Ileana, according to her lawyer, received a visit in her darkened solitary cell from an intimidating and burly 6 feet 2 inches-tall woman. The woman told Ileana that she *knew* that Ileana and her husband were guilty. But how can that be: We are innocent, Ileana proclaimed. Who are you? "I'm Janet Reno," the woman said. Ileana repeatedly told Reno that she was innocent, and Reno kept repeating, "I'm sorry, but you are not. You're going to have to help us." Reno made several more solitary, nightly visits to the naked Ileana, each time threatening Ileana that she would remain in prison for the rest of her life if she didn't tell Reno what she wanted to hear.

Finally, Reno hired two psychiatrists from a company called Behavior Changers Inc., who met with Ileana thirty-four times in a one-month period. These psychiatrists claimed to be able to help individuals "recover memories," but their technique was simply to hypnotize Ileana so that she could be brainwashed into believing that Frank Fuster was a child molester. The coercion eventually worked; with the psychiatrists present and with Janet Reno *squeezing her hand*, Ileana implicated her husband.

Ileana's trial testimony against her husband put the final nail in Frank Fuster's coffin. Reno won the conviction, her reelection bid, her name in newspaper headlines, and a stepping stone to a position as the nation's chief law enforcement officer. However, Ileana Fuster has repeatedly retracted her confession and testimony, swearing that she and Fuster never abused any of the children and that her confession was the product of brainwashing.

Yet, thanks to Janet Reno, an innocent Fuster remains incarcerated for the rest of his life.

3

CREATING CRIME

The practice of police entrapment is a perversion of the policing function, which should be to deter the bad guys by police presence or to catch the bad guys when a crime has been committed. "Entrapment" is to law enforcement what "practice development" is to the legal profession. It's a business builder. "Not enough crime to keep us busy," or "someone we need to get off the street," the police might say. "Well, let's stimulate some crime by tossing out a lure or two. Let's create some 'business.'"

Yes, it sounds absurd. Isn't there enough "legitimate crime" (interesting phrase, that) to keep our police busy? Apparently not, as I can attest from my own experience.

WORKING UNDERCOVER

Frequently I attend Mass on Sundays at a Roman Catholic church on Washington Square Park in New York City. I was walking out of that church one Sunday morning, having just ingested the Blessed Sacrament. I cut through the park, and among parents and children this scruffy guy hounded me, offering marijuana by saying, "Smoke? Smoke?"

After four or five times, I turned to him and said, basically, "Get lost." At that point, the "drug dealer" drew himself up and flipped over his coat's lapel to reveal his NYPD badge. "Have a good day, your honor," he said and then melted into the crowd.

To say I was fuming is an understatement. But there was nothing I could do. He knew me. The undercover policeman/drug dealer and his crew had been assigned to this part of Manhattan for the day, and it cost them nothing to take a run at me. I was probably their main amusement for that particular hour of their shift. (Question: Why wasn't the *cop* prosecuted for attempting to sell drugs?)

Apparently New York City police officials feel that they can disregard the Constitution when they are trying to clean up Washington Square Park. No matter how noble and well intentioned the city's efforts may be, those intentions do not give them a license to infringe upon constitutionally guaranteed liberties. The Constitution ensures that we live in a free society, and our society will go to shambles if the police are allowed to use Gestapo-like tactics to apprehend criminals.

In the months leading up to former Mayor Rudolph W. Guliani's re-election campaign, the New York City Police Department's Narcotics Division led a four-month undercover investigation of repeat drug offenders. Guliani vowed to make Washington Square Park—which was once a notorious haven for drug dealers—a drug-free zone. The city was faced with the difficulty of marijuana dealers who kept returning to the park after serving short jail sentences.

On June 19, 1997, Lloyd G. McNeil found himself at the wrong place at the wrong time. McNeil, age sixty-two, a Rutgers University professor, was sitting on a bench in Washington Square Park with a group of people his age. That day, undercover police officers began a sweep of the park: they entered the area to buy marijuana and to arrest suspected dealers as they left.

Toward the end of the day, the police set up barricades to seal off all of the exits for the park. They illegally prevented *everyone* from leaving. McNeil, who had a 5:30 P.M. appointment across the park at New York University with a graduate student who was scheduled to defend her thesis before him, got up and walked to a park exit at about 5:20. A police officer told McNeil that he could not leave until the raid was over and informed him, "If you come around that barrier, I'll handcuff you and arrest you." McNeil decided to walk around the barrier and was punched and pushed in the chest by the police officer before being pushed yet again, and then ultimately handcuffed. He was detained in a patrol car before being released by a higher-ranking officer.

McNeil was not the only law-abiding citizen who happened to be in the park that afternoon. Joseph Rubin, a retired writer who was walking his dog in the park during the sweep, told the *New York Times*, "They were saying no one could leave. There were a lot of mothers with baby carriages and small children. There were students trying to get back to class. There was a mass of people at the exit," and the police prevented them all from leaving a public place.

Police department officials were quick to defend their actions and were lauded by New Yorkers who apparently were never falsely imprisoned in a public park, residents who were thrilled to see the police clean up the place. Deputy Inspector Michael Mandel explained that everyone was "fed up with the continued sale of narcotics over the years" and that taking out the drug dealers in the sweep "should break the back of the problem in the park."

The police certainly provided local residents—of which I was one— with a significant benefit. But at what cost?

Mandel stated that he was not aware of *any* complaints from people who were not able to leave the park and explained that sealing the park was "the most efficient way to round up the dealers." Clearly, Mandel forgot about Lloyd McNeil—a professor in his sixties punched, pushed, and handcuffed by the police—and all of the students and mothers with babies. Pardon the pun, but the cops threw out the baby with bath water. Efficiency does not override the Constitution, and the police department's operations must conform to the law. Professor McNeil has the right to enter and leave a public park whenever he wants. The police cannot, at their whim, arrest an individual who has done nothing more than be present at particular place at a particular time. When the Nazis were engaged in their vicious racial pogroms, they frequently rounded up all persons in a town square, until they found the "law-breakers" among them. Heaven help those who left before the police gave permission.

Aren't cops sworn to uphold the law? The U.S. Supreme Court, in the 1972 case of *Papachristou v. City of Jacksonville* and the 1969 case of *Shapiro v. Thomson*, articulated McNeil's freedom of movement as a fundamental—that is, a natural—right. The government may only override fundamental rights when a compelling state interest is addressed by the most narrrowly tailored means. I would argue that arresting a drug dealer in Washington Square Park is not really a compelling state interest, but even if it were, the police had no right to restrict McNeil's movement and prevent him from leaving the park because falsely imprisoning every person within Washington Square Park was clearly *not* the most narrowly tailored means to serve that governmental interest. The police trampled on far more human liberty than was justified by their desire to round up a few pot dealers. It was an unquestionable violation of McNeil's constitutional liberties for the police to arrest him solely on the basis of being at a particular place.

Local residents should have been outraged that they could have found themselves being punched and handcuffed because they were in the park that afternoon. While they should have been happy that the police alleviated the park's drug-dealing problem, it is un-American to give the police a "free pass" to commit crimes in order prevent further crimes. A sergeant told Professor McNeil, "If you come to the park regularly, you know that drug dealing has gotten out of hand. You can appreciate what we're trying to do." Citizens should condemn—not appreciate—the police when they so blatantly ignore guaranteed liberties.

MESSING WITH TEXANS

It is unfair, unwise, and un-American for police to break the law in order to enforce it, and Gestapo-like police tactics are not limited to Washington Square Park. A corrupt police officer in Tulia, Texas, a small rural town of five thousand people, engaged in what one commentator deemed an "ethnic cleansing of young male blacks."

Thomas Coleman, an undercover narcotics officer, committed one of the worst police atrocities in recent years by arresting forty-six people on July 23, 1999. Thirty-nine of those arrested were black, which amounts to approximately half of the town's adult black population. Many others were involved in family or personal relationships with black Americans in an otherwise overwhelmingly white community. Coleman's previous law enforcement employers knew that Coleman himself had once been arrested for theft during an undercover operation, that he used racial epithets, and that he had a widespread reputation in the Texas law enforcement community as being unreliable and untrustworthy.

Nonetheless, on the basis of Coleman's testimony, thirty-eight individuals arrested on that day were found to be guilty of drug dealing. Some were sentenced to up to ninety years in prison! Some were coerced into accepting plea bargains under the threat of lengthy imprisonment.

What is most shocking is that the prosecution's *only evidence* against these defendants was the testimony of Coleman, the dirty cop. The testimony was uncorroborated: no witnesses or other police officers could confirm that Coleman bought drugs from these defendants. And, Coleman could not offer any audio or video surveillance verifying his undercover drug purchases. Not even fingerprint evidence was introduced.

Coleman's testimony was solely based on notes he scribbled on his stomach and his leg. He did not keep a permanent notebook. At the time of their arrests, these forty-six supposed drug dealers possessed no guns, no drugs, and no money. Coleman claimed to have purchased twenty-thousand-dollars worth of cocaine from these "dealers." Furthermore, some of the individuals who were arrested established that they were miles away from Tulia that day. A few of them neither worked nor lived in Tulia. All of the people arrested that day were either convicted by juries or pleaded guilty. In 1999, Texas Attorney General John Cornyn—now a U.S. senator—named Coleman the outstanding law enforcement officer of the year.

Two friends of mine who represented Tulia defendants in post-conviction *habeas corpus* proceedings said one of their clients had time-punch cards proving he was at work at the time Coleman alleged to have purchased drugs from him in another part of the city. Another Tulia defendant was able to clear her name only after she was able to produce ATM receipts showing she was at a bank in another state at the time Coleman claimed to have engaged in a drug transaction with her in Tulia. These individuals were fortunate enough to have incontrovertible documentary proof that they were not where Tom Coleman claimed they were at the time he claimed to have engaged in a drug transaction with them. Just imagine how difficult it was for some of the other minority, low-income defendants in Tulia to imagine that they could produce the proofs needed to counter-balance the testimony of a police officer, and imagine how willing they might have been to plead guilty to a lesser jail term after they saw some of their also-innocent neighbors sentenced to up to ninety years based solely on the "evidence" provided by a law-breaking, slip-shod, racist cop.

The Tulia, Texas, debacle attracted national media attention and a coordinated multi-defendant *habeas corpus* campaign, coordinated by the NAACP and many law firms. About four years later, the Texas Court of Criminal Appeals exonerated the victims of Coleman's fraud. Coleman had previously acknowledged that the convictions were based on nothing more than his testimony. While he stated that he was "pretty sure" that all the defendants "deserved" to be behind bars, he admitted to several "mess ups" and stated that some of his own sworn testimony was "questionable." It is a rare anomaly that police abuses such as that perpetrated in Tulia, Texas, are overturned. You can't help but wonder how many wrongfully convicted defendants never had the luxury of seeing justice served. It shouldn't be a luxury.

Coleman currently faces trial for perjury, but the buck does not stop at Thomas Coleman. Coleman's activities were financed by the federal government's war on drugs, as he was part of the Panhandle Regional Narcotics Task Force. The Department of Justice encourages officers like

Coleman to rack up as many arrests as possible, since money is allocated to the task forces based on the number of *arrests*, not *convictions*. Because there is no distinction between high-quality and low-level arrests, the federal government creates an incentive for officers like Coleman to engage in sloppy investigations against low-level offenders, and against the innocent.

The Texas prosecutors, who blatantly disregarded their responsibilities, must also be held accountable for these horrible incidents. Terry McEachern, who prosecuted all of the cases, is currently under investigation by the State Bar of Texas. It is alleged that McEachern withheld evidence from the defense about Coleman's background, misrepresented evidence during the trial, and failed to turn over any evidence that was favorable to the defense. Prosecutorial discretion is the essence of the criminal justice system, and McEachern had the duty and responsibility not to prosecute a case when it was so likely that his sole witness fabricated the entire scheme. At a minimum, McEachern had a duty to turn over to defense attorneys evidence of Coleman's prior personal, criminal, and other dubious behavior that spoke to his credibility as a witness against the many individuals who were tried and convicted based solely on Coleman's testimony.

COOKING CONVICTIONS

Sometimes law enforcement officers decide that a small town needs ethnic cleansing, while other times officers decide to manufacture highly illicit drugs like methamphetamine and blame it on small town folks.

Joe Shapiro, an undercover agent for the Federal Bureau of Narcotics and Dangerous Drugs, was assigned to locate a laboratory where he believed methamphetamine was illegally being manufactured. He decided that if he couldn't locate one, he'd create one.

At the time of Agent Shapiro's misdeeds, phenyl-2-propanone, the essential ingredient in the manufacture of methamphetamine, was indisputably difficult to obtain. The chemical could only be purchased with a license, and the federal government had recently requested that suppliers not sell to people *even with a license to purchase*. Because only the government could obtain the chemical, it would have been extraordinarily difficult for a private individual to manufacture meth. So why was the government looking for a nonexistent laboratory?

Agent Shapiro went to Whidbey Island, Washington, and knocked on the door of Richard Russell's home on December 7, 1969. Shapiro told Russell that he represented an organization in the Pacific Northwest that was interested in controlling the manufacture and distribution of methamphetamine. Shapiro and Russell agreed to a deal, whereby Shapiro would supply the essential phenyl-2-propanone chemical in exchange for one-half of the drug produced.

Two days later, Agent Shapiro *delivered the chemical* to Russell's laboratory. Shapiro stayed and watched the entire manufacturing process. He even *assisted in the process* by placing aluminum foil pieces into a flask. The following day, Shapiro received half of the drug. He also *purchased* part of the remainder from Russell for sixty dollars.

The following month, Agent Shapiro returned with a search warrant for the laboratory and arrested Russell. A jury convicted Russell of having unlawfully manufactured, processed, sold, and delivered methamphetamine. The U.S. Court of Appeals for the Ninth Circuit reversed the conviction because there was "an intolerable degree of governmental participation" in Russell's crime. However, by a five-to-four margin, the U.S. Supreme Court condoned the government's illegal entrapment and reinstated Russell's conviction.

"It is the government's duty to prevent crime, not promote it," Justice Potter Stewart wrote in dissent.

Sometimes it is necessary for the government to engage in undercover operations, particularly when it is trying to solve victimless crimes. However, the line is clearly drawn—and it becomes entrapment—when the government goes so far that it is instigating someone to commit a crime, that is, actually planting the seed of illegal acts in the person's brain in order to prosecute the instigated person for committing the crime.

Agent Shapiro's behavior was a textbook example of entrapment. Shapiro commissioned Russell to produce an illegal drug for him. Shapiro promised to supply an essential ingredient that Russell could not have obtained on his own. Shapiro furnished the ingredient as promised, performed a role in the manufacturing process, and bought the finished product. Why wasn't *he* prosecuted for manufacturing and purchasing drugs?

A majority of the Supreme Court ignored the Constitution's requirement of due process and couldn't find that Shapiro's scheme constituted entrapment. Chief Justice Rehnquist—Justice Rehnquist at the time—reasoned that Russell was predisposed to selling methamphetamine and would have committed the crime even without Shapiro supplying the essential chemical. This argument totally ignored the fact that phenyl-2-propanone was so difficult to obtain, that Russell would not have been able to manufacture the drug on his own. As Justice Stewart asked, "If the chemical was so easily available elsewhere, then why did not [Agent Shapiro] simply wait until [Russell] had himself obtained the ingredients and produced the drug, and then buy it from him?" The answer is pretty clear: when it comes to law enforcement, logic and individual rights mean very little.

LIGHTS! CAMERA! TYRANNY!

Sometimes the government will choose more subtle, but equally shocking, methods to deprive you of your constitutional rights. Cities and municipalities determine that they could use a little extra cash, so they implement traffic enforcement cameras at major intersections. These "scameras," upon determining that you commit a red light infraction, take a picture of your car and mail you a citation. These cameras do not increase public safety; they only allow the government to convict you illegally of a crime that you may not have committed.

Take San Diego, California, a city that in 1998 was in need of $100 million for maintenance of roads and other public works. In 1998, San Diego officials entered into a contract with Lockheed Martin IMS Corp. Lockheed Martin paid for the installation of nineteen cameras, and operated the system. San Diego would receive $271 for each traffic conviction, of which Lockheed Martin would receive $70. So the manufacturer had a financial incentive to create a camera designed not only to capture speeders, but also to convict them.

In eighteen months, one camera alone generated $6.8 million in revenue. Given such incentive, it's no big surprise that testimony presented to the House Subcommittee on Highways and Safety revealed the city's traffic camera program was a complete scam intended only for increased revenues, concocted "under the guise of public safety."

Lockheed Martin and San Diego claimed that the cameras would save lives, but not a single report substantiates this claim. Of the thousands of photos taken by Lockheed Martin's cameras, not a single photo shows a red light violator causing a collision.

Shockingly, officials from Lockheed Martin, not from San Diego, chose the intersections for the nineteen cameras. Lockheed Martin selected the locations not based on safety, but on revenue potential. Not only did Lockheed Martin have an incentive to issue more citations, but the contract also allowed its officials to remove the camera from an intersection when there was a 25 percent decrease in the number of citations issued.

It was later determined that, at three intersections, Lockheed Martin illegally moved the censor that measures whether the car crosses into the intersection during a red light so as *to increase the likelihood* of a conviction.

Numerous studies show that the most effective way to reduce red light violations—and traffic accidents—is to increase the yellow light interval. When one San Diego intersection's yellow light interval was increased from 3.0 to 4.7 seconds, the number of monthly red light violations dropped from 2,265 to 205! As former San Diego Mayor Roger Hedgecock testified to Congress, there was "not a single scrap of evidence that one life has been saved" by the cameras. Additionally, Hedgecock explained that San Diego was "contracting out law enforcement [to private, for-profit, corporations]. Outrageous."

Americans have an inalienable right to life, liberty, and property; the government may not strip individuals of these rights without due process. In San Diego, the government devised an elaborate and devious scheme to convict harmless and innocent people. When the yellow light interval becomes so small that it is inevitable that you will run a red light, as was the case at some San Diego intersections, the government is entrapping you: it is *facilitating* and *inducing* you to the break the law. If the government caused the duration of the yellow light to become one second or less, it would be *forcing* you to commit a crime! With no fair process whatsoever, the government has deprived drivers in San Diego of their liberty (by convicting them of a crime) and their property (by robbing them of $271 per citation).

The judiciary has not acted as an effective check on law enforcement's use of scameras. In 2001, three hundred violators had their citations dismissed by San Diego Superior Court Judge Ronald Styn, who ruled that a private company had too much involvement, and the city had too little involvement, in the process. In other words, *the government* was not enforcing the law, *Lockheed Martin* was. Sadly, Judge Styn is a rare exception.

While cameras don't lie, government officials do. A driver who is automatically mailed a red light violation has no effective way of establishing that the government rigged the system. The Sixth Amendment guarantees the right to confront one's accuser. How can an individual cross-examine the camera? While an individual can certainly spend numerous hours reviewing traffic documentation and reports to prove his innocence, the government knows that most individuals have not the time, ability, or money to do so. So, the government collects a little $271 check from you, when you did little wrong, and there is little you can do about it!

EXTREME AND OUTRAGEOUS

Emboldened by its victory in the case over alleged methamphetamine producer Richard Russell, the federal government had no qualms about taking extreme and outrageous steps to apprehend and incarcerate a harmless and innocent citizen.

Keith Jacobson, a Vietnam War veteran and a Nebraska farmer, found himself the target of a twenty-six-month government sting. From January 1985 to March 1987, the U.S. Postal Service and the Customs Service concocted five fictitious organizations and a bogus pen pal in order to trap Jacobson into breaking the new child pornography law.

In 1984, Jacobson ordered and received, from an adult bookstore in California, two magazines containing images of nude preteen and teenage boys. At that time, Jacobson's actions were legal under both state and federal law. Soon thereafter, Congress passed a law that criminalized the receipt of child pornography in the mail. Having found Jacobson's name on the California adult bookstore's mailing list, the postal inspectors sought to induce Jacobson into breaking the newly created child pornography law.

The government's tactics began in January 1985, when a U.S. postal inspector sent Jacobson a letter through the U.S. mail from the "American Hedonist Society," which was a sham organization. The letter included literature about the "right to read what we desire," and asked Jacobson to complete a sexual attitude questionnaire.

A year later, another U.S. postal inspector, whose job title was "prohibited mailing specialist," created a fictitious consumer research company, "Midlands Data Research," and mailed a survey to Jacobson. The survey sought responses from people who believed in the "joys of sex and the complete awareness of those lusty and youthful lads and lasses of the neophyte age."

A third sham organization, "Heartland Institute for a New Tomorrow," (HINT) initiated contact with Jacobson, stating that its purpose was "to protect freedom and promote sexual freedom and freedom of choice." Jacobson responded to the HINT survey by stating that he had an above average interest in "preteen sex-homosexual material." HINT then replied that it was a lobbying organization seeking to end governmental regulation of sexual activities, whose efforts were funded by sales from a catalog offering items "which we believe you will find to be both interesting and stimulating." The postal inspector also used the guise of HINT to send three pen-pal letters to Jacobson under the pseudonym of "Carl Long."

After striking out for more than two years, the postal inspectors realized they had no evidence that Jacobson had violated the child pornography law. So, a Customs Service agent began communicating to Jacobson through a fictitious company called "Product Outaouais." The Customs inspector mailed to Jacobson a brochure advertising photographs of young boys engaging in sex. Additionally, the postal inspectors began a new campaign against Jacobson, posing as the "Far Eastern Trading Company." The postal inspectors mailed a letter stating that they had "devised a method of getting these to you without prying eyes of U.S. Customs seizing your mail," and asked Jacobson to sign that he was not a government official "entrapping Far Eastern Trading Company." After receiving a catalog from the federal agents, Jacobson finally succumbed and ordered a magazine containing child pornography.

Blatantly violating the child pornography law they were sworn to enforce, the U.S. postal inspectors actually mailed and delivered the child pornography to Jacobson.

Distributing child pornography through the U.S. mail wasn't the only crime that the government agents committed. It is also a federal crime to send a fraudulent device or document through the U.S. mail. In their pursuit of Jacobson, the government violated this criminal law at least eight times. Got that? *The government committed at least nine federal crimes in order to induce Jacobson to commit just one.* What possibly was accomplished by the government's endless and illegal pursuit of Jacobson?

Jacobson was arrested, tried, and convicted. Whatever geniuses in the government devised this scheme had invested so much time and money in it that they had to see it to a desirable end. But the Constitution was waiting for them! Jacobson's conviction was upheld on appeal. Then a divided U.S. Supreme Court voted five-to-four to free him. A man with no guilty intention, who was merely a victim of overreaching government criminal agents, was one Supreme Court justice's vote away from imprisonment for twenty years.

Entrapment is law enforcement by trickery and deceit, and is a complete defense to a criminal prosecution. This was exactly Jacobson's situation, since the government used criminal means to taunt, tease, and browbeat an innocent—albeit naïve—man to commit a crime that he had no intention of committing.

There are limits to the government's ability to enforce the law. As Justice Byron White wrote, the government may not "originate a criminal design, implant in an innocent man's mind the disposition to commit a criminal act, and then induce commission of the crime so that the government may prosecute."

The techniques that the law forbids are exactly what the government used in its efforts to trap Jacobson. Even though he had inclinations toward child pornography, he had never previously violated the child pornography law, and the Supreme Court found that he would not have, but for the government's involvement. He had absolutely no intention of breaking the law until he finally broke down after the government's twenty-six-month-long effort to induce him to do so. When Jacobson was arrested, the government searched his house and found nothing criminal or incriminating except what the government had sent him and the magazine that he purchased legally in 1984. The law protects innocent people—even those with weaknesses—and bars the government from exploiting these weaknesses in order to induce people to commit crimes.

NET STINGS

Despite Jacobson's victory at the Supreme Court, the government continues to entrap individuals it fears may commit crimes. In Westchester County, New York, District Attorney Jeanine Pirro oversees a "High Technology Crimes Bureau," which is a vehicle to entrap individuals the government fears might be pedophiles. District Attorney Pirro's office has arrested and convicted over seventy individuals—deemed pedophiles and child pornographers—whether or not those individuals had actually committed a crime.

If the government is afraid that a particular individual might be a pedophile, it will use trickery to arrest that individual, even if no crime was committed. In a typical undercover Internet sting operation, a law enforcement officer poses as a minor and engages in a "conversation" with the suspected pedophile.

In one typical case, a Westchester County investigator impersonated a fourteen-year-old girl and began a conversation with Steve Paravati, age forty-seven. In his conversations with the undercover investigator, Paravati described sexual acts that he sought to perform on the "girl." Paravati arranged to meet the "girl" and was promptly arrested when he arrived at the meeting spot.

Paravati was charged with having an explicit *conversation* with a minor. Legislatures enact such laws so that it is easier for the police to arrest people in violation of the Constitution: How can it be a crime to have an anonymous conversation about sex? Who and where was the minor? These statutes are a complete insult and direct contradiction to the First Amendment, as they punish the defendant for his thoughts and words ("Congress shall make no law . . . abridging the freedom of speech") not his acts. Numerous other individuals have been charged with similar offenses. Not only did Paravati never sexually harm the "girl," but also it would have been impossible for him to do so because he had arranged to meet an adult male police officer, not a fourteen-year-old girl. There is no evidence that Paravati had previously harmed any other minors, or else he would have been charged with those offenses, so the government had to invent a persona in order to lure an innocent man into a guilty mindset. Not only is this textbook entrapment, but Paravati's actions were well short of criminal. Jacobson eventually ordered child pornography, but Paravati never even *met* any minor! The government merely feared that he *might* meet one and commit a crime in the future, so it invented a crime for him now.

TERROR TRAPS

In our technological world, the Internet is not only being used to entrap potential pedophiles but also to entrap individuals who have the potential to become terrorists. And, private citizens—as well as police officers— have begun to take the law into their own hands with the government's blessings in order to track down these potential terrorists.

Shannen Rossmiller, a paralegal turned "citizen spy," is a member of a group called 7-Seas Global Intelligence Security Team. The group's mission is to provide the government with terrorist information and intelligence. Members of the group visit Islamic Web sites, chat rooms, and bulletin boards, where they impersonate Middle Eastern men and try to communicate with radical Muslims and jihad warriors.

Rossmiller came across a posting on bravemuslim.com by a man calling himself "Amir Abdul Rashid," who was "edging toward violence." Rossmiller posed as an Algerian with ties to a militant Islamic group and sent "Rashid" an email entitled "A Call to Jihad." "Rashid" responded by asking whether a "brother fighting on the wrong side could defect." After she exchanged twenty-seven emails with "Rashid" over a four-month period, Rossmiller learned that "Rashid" was really a U.S. National Guardsman about to be deployed in Iraq.

She reported "Rashid" to the government, since he appeared to be willing to share information on American troop vulnerabilities with the enemy.

This information led to the arrest of "Rashid," who was actually Ryan Anderson, age twenty-seven, a specialist in the Washington National Guard. Rossmiller was the star witness at Anderson's court martial for attempting to aid and provide intelligence to the enemy. Who did Anderson harm?

The government, or private citizens like Rossmiller who are operating as agents of the government, overreaches its law enforcement power when it arrests individuals without their having committed any crime. Before Rossmiller entrapped him, nothing suggests that Anderson had any intent to share military strategies with the enemy; and intent alone is not criminal—acting on the intent is.

Rossmiller preyed on an individual who was innocent. Merely "edging toward violence" is not a crime. She exchanged twenty emails with him until she caused him to make an "incriminating" statement. Had Rossmiller never communicated with Anderson and provoked him, it is quite possible that Anderson would never have reached a state where he was willing to share troop vulnerabilities with the enemy. Not only did the government illegally entrap Anderson, but the government itself could have harmed U.S. troops by provoking and coercing one of its own soldiers to reach a stage where he would be willing to aid the enemy.

On September 3, 2004, after he was convicted by a court martial, Anderson was sentenced to life in prison. The crime was attempted treason. Who did he harm?

IN THE STATE'S CLUTCHES

What lesson can be learned from all of this? Once the government invests the time and money to trap you, it will not stop. When it gets in so deeply that lawful means can no longer trap you, it will literally break the law in order to enforce the law. And if there is no law that criminalizes your conduct, it will create one. What can these government agents think of the oaths they swore to uphold the law?

4

GRABBING GUNS,
ENDANGERING CITIZENS

The right to possess arms is a fundamental human right. This right is *guaranteed* in the Second Amendment, which states that "[a] well regulated Militia, being necessary to the security of a free state, the right of the people to keep and bear arms, shall not be infringed."

Contrary to popular political beliefs, the right to possess a firearm has little to do with hunting or any other recreational activity. The basic right to possess a gun serves a much more important function in our society: self-defense. The right has two purposes: It allows individuals to protect themselves from criminals when the government is *unable to protect* them. Even more importantly, the right exists so that individuals can protect themselves *from the government* when it unjustly attacks them.

Over the last hundred years, federal and state governments have engaged in a direct assault on the right to possess firearms. Legislators have enacted law after law in order to eradicate the right slowly. These so-called gun controls make it extraordinarily difficult for a law-abiding individual to obtain a weapon and nearly impossible for that person to carry and actually to use the weapon in self-defense.

The Supreme Court has refused to step in and reaffirm the peoples' right to arm themselves for the purpose of self-defense, as it has not decided *a single case* on Second Amendment grounds since 1939. In that year, the Court issued an ambiguous and convoluted opinion in the case of *United States v. Miller* that ducked the issue of whether the Constitution guarantees a private person's fundamental right to own and use firearms.

When the government strips persons of their right to protect themselves and gets away with it, a dangerous precedent is established. America is spiraling downward on a slippery slope toward a defenseless population.

DISARMING THE PEOPLE

Judge Alex Kozinski, a great jurist and member of the U.S. Court of Appeals for the Ninth Circuit, expressed concern over the disarming of America in a staunch dissent in the 2003 case of *Silveira v. Lockyer.* Explaining how "tyranny thrives best where government need not fear the wrath of an armed people," Judge Kozinski documented the world's greatest atrocities, all of which were "perpetrated by armed troops against unarmed populations."

While a disarmed population doesn't necessarily lead to a genocidal government, not a single incident of genocide in the twentieth century was inflicted on an armed population. The state and federal governments assert that they are well intentioned, yet they ignore the history that a defenseless citizenry is easy to exterminate. The Founding Fathers certainly recognized and feared that possibility. "However improbable these contingencies may seem today," Judge Kozinski wrote, "[t]he Second Amendment is a doomsday provision." Certainly nobody could have predicted the slaughter of six million individuals during the Holocaust. Who knows what is next?

After World War I, the pacifist and idealistic liberals of the Weimar Republic in Germany—and other governments in war-ravaged Europe—decided to disarm their citizens in order to quell the violence and rebellion that was taking place on the streets. This framework made it easy for the Nazis to rise to power over a defenseless nation. Once Adolf Hitler took over, the Nazis specifically forbade Jews from owning guns or any other weapon, and exempted members of the Sturmabteilung, Hitler's paramilitary organization, and Nazi party members from the existing gun laws.

As the fateful Kristallnact incident on November 9, 1937, demonstrates, a defenseless people simply can't rely on the government's "we're here to protect you" mantra. That night, in a nationwide uprising against the Jews, German mobs assaulted and killed hundreds of people, burned synagogues, and smashed countless shops and homes. These victims, unarmed and unable to defend against these attacks, were forced to rely on the government to defend them. But according to German national police chief Hermann Goering, "the police protect whoever comes into German legitimacy, but not Jewish usurers." As Kristallnacht demonstrated, when the government disarms its citizenry, it deprives its population of the basic human right to defend themselves.

The Warsaw Ghetto uprising in April 1943, on the other hand, demonstrates the difficulty of committing genocide against an armed population. One day, without notice, two thousand Wehrmacht troops arrived in the Jewish ghetto in Warsaw, Poland, in military tanks and armed with machine guns. Their orders were to liquidate the remaining Jewish population and transport survivors to the concentration camps. Surprisingly they met resistance from a loosely organized group of Zionists, the Jewish Combat Organization (ZOB). The ZOB was sparsely equipped, as it had seized small arms and grenades from Gestapo agents who previously tried to raid Warsaw.

With only small arms and grenades, the ZOB was able to kill about three hundred members of the highly trained and equipped Nazi military. And these brave men of the ZOB were able to hold off the Nazis for almost a month! Some escaped, others committed suicide; not a single one of these fighters was carted off to the concentration camps.

Imagine if Europe's Jewish population never had their weapons confiscated by those idealistic socialists of the Weimar Republic and other interwar governments. Had the Jews in Warsaw been adequately rather than sparsely armed, how long would it have taken the Nazis to defeat the Jewish resistance? As the Warsaw uprisings illustrate, if the rest of the European Jews were not stripped of their basic human right to defend themselves against a genocidal government, the Nazis would have had an extraordinarily difficult time carting off six million of them. While it is unlikely that an armed Jewish population would have been able to avoid the Holocaust entirely, historians agree that the magnitude of deaths would have been greatly diminished had Jews been able to resist Nazi capture and defend themselves. And if the Nazis had to redirect significant military forces to rounding up the Jews, how could they have effectively held off the approaching Allies from the West and Russians from the East until mid-1945?

PRELUDE TO GENOCIDE

A genocidal government, as well as an idealistic government, will seek to disarm its population. In the 1970s, the Khmer Rouge—the communist government in Cambodia—slaughtered at least two million people (about 30 percent of population) in a four-year period. The Khmer Rouge's disorganized army of merely a hundred thousand could never have accomplished such a massacre against an armed population. They recognized that.

"We are here now to protect you, and no one has a need for a weapon anymore," a soldier told a Cambodian citizen (who survived the slaughter). Under the friendly guise of communitarianism, the military confiscated all of the citizenry's weapons by undertaking a hut-to-hut search of the entire nation. Virtually everyone was forced to step aside while the soldiers rampaged their dwellings to find their weapons. And when the government concluded that the population was no longer armed, the massacres began.

In the twentieth century, numerous other genocides were perpetrated on defenseless populations. The Turks systematically disarmed the Armenians in the early 1900s, and then proceeded to kill at least one million of them. On a positive note, Armenians in the Aleppo province were able to resist two different sets of Turkish forces before the British evacuated them. Of course, these Armenians had secretly possessed weapons. Each of these genocides against unarmed civilians is strikingly similar, including the Soviet Union, China, Rwanda, Indonesia, Uganda, Iran, Iraq, and Sudan, to name a few. History clearly teaches us why bearing arms is a fundamental human right.

Naysayers would like to believe, "never in America." Compare the mantra of the Khmer Rouge ("we are here now to protect you, and no one has a need for a weapon anymore") to President Ronald Reagan's famous quip, "The nine most terrifying words in the English language are, 'I'm from the government and I'm here to help.'" Oppression over an unarmed and defenseless population can happen anywhere. And, for the record, it *has* happened in America.

THE ATTACK ON BLACKS

In the Antebellum period, the Southern states went to great lengths to ensure that blacks—both slaves and free—remained unarmed and defenseless against the government. Despite the fact that slaves were unable to own property, there existed specific disarmament statutes whereby slave masters would conduct weapons searches. And, in 1857, when the U.S. Supreme Court, in the case of *Dred Scott v. Sandford,* infamously ruled that blacks could never become American citizens, Chief Justice Roger B. Taney wrote that citizenship "would give to persons of the Negro race . . . the right to . . . keep and carry arms wherever they went." Undoubtedly, fundamental to tyranny and oppression is the oppressor's destruction of the victims' rights to protect themselves. If Southern blacks had been armed and able to fight for their freedom, perhaps we would never have had to fight the Civil War.

Immediately after the Civil War, Southern governments, at the behest of the newly-formed Ku Klux Klan, enacted Black Codes to prohibit the freed slaves from owning and bearing firearms. These provisions made blacks defenseless against violent crimes perpetrated by the Klan and other racist groups, who were neither punished nor disarmed after committing these atrocities.

Congress and the states recognized that possessing arms was among the most fundamental of all human rights and enacted the Fourteenth Amendment in 1868 to alleviate the terror against blacks. The Fourteenth Amendment made most of the protections of the Bill of Rights—including the Second Amendment right to keep and bear arms—apply against the overreaching state governments. Once the Fourteenth Amendment passed, "Congress shall make no law" came to mean "Congress and the states shall make no law."

Not that it was adequately enforced. In the early twentieth century, as waves of immigrants entered America and as the children and grandchildren of slaves began to seek equal rights, the Second Ku Klux Klan and other racist mobs flourished. Recognizing that social control over minorities was synonymous with the deprivation of gun rights, the Klan influenced Southern states to enact firearms licensing programs. But it didn't stop there. These gun controls spread to the North, including New York, which enacted handgun prohibitions that were expressly designed to disarm blacks, Italians, Jews, and other immigrant groups.

When the right of self-defense is denied, an oppressive government possesses the ability to make an ethnic minority defenseless against an oppressive and tyrannical group of armed individuals. The Second Amendment is designed to prevent this exact sort of atrocity, since it is impossible to foresee the next Holocaust; and it is impossible to foresee if the next Holocaust will come at the hands of the government itself or those whom the government cannot or will not restrain.

BEARING ARMS: AN INDIVIDUAL RIGHT

In recent years, the power-hungry state and federal governments and collectivist judges have rendered almost meaningless the Second

Amendment's guarantee that "the right of the people to keep and bear arms shall not be infringed."

These governmental institutions have used the amendment's militia clause ("a well regulated Militia, being necessary to the security of a free state . . .") to pervert the Second Amendment into becoming a "collective right." Under this absurd "collective right" theory, the Second Amendment has nothing to do with personal or individual rights but somehow guarantees a state's power to maintain a military establishment, like the state police or the National Guard.

The Second Amendment clearly guarantees *an individual's right* to keep and bear arms; to state otherwise ignores the words of the Constitution and almost two hundred years of Supreme Court rulings. The Second Amendment plainly states that the right to keep and bear arms is "*the right of the people.*" Under the Constitution, state governments have "powers" or "authorit[ies]" but never "rights." Only individuals have "rights."

Furthermore, the "*right* of the people" phrase appears *four times* in the Bill of Rights, and each time it clearly represents an individual's rights against the government, a *guarantee* that the government cannot take away. It is ludicrous to think that the Founding Fathers used "right of the people" in the First Amendment (sixteen words earlier) and in the Fourth Amendment (forty-six words later) to refer to individual rights, yet meant something totally different when they used those *exact same words* in the Second Amendment.

And how can a state possibly "bear arms"? The phrase "bear arms," according to a 1998 U.S. Supreme Court ruling, describes an individual carrying a firearm. While a state can certainly own arms, the ability to "bear arms" is something that only a human being can do.

The Founding Fathers unquestionably believed the Second Amendment would guarantee an individual's right to self-defense. The militia clause ("a well regulated Militia, being necessary to the security of a free state . . .") expresses the proposition that the entire law-abiding and adult population of individually armed citizens comprised the state's militia. Since the Constitution prohibits states from maintaining standing armies without congressional consent, the state's militia is nothing more than the law-abiding, gun-owning adults that make up its citizenry.

The existence of militia laws—*requirements* that every household be armed in order to ensure the defense of the home and the overall community—in the colonial period further supports the notion that the arms of the militia are merely the arms of individual persons within a particular state. To maintain otherwise—that the Second Amendment protects the arms of the state but not the arms of its individual citizens—stems from a nonsensical interpretation of American history.

HALLMARK OF FREEDOM

The Founding Fathers undoubtedly recognized that an armed citizenry is the hallmark of a free society. Even centuries ago, Aristotle declared that tyrannies "mistrust the people and therefore deprive them of their arms." During the constitutional debates, the idea of denying Americans the right to possess arms was unheard of. Second Amendment scholar Donald B. Kates has documented that, while there was much ideological disagreement on many issues between the Federalists and the Anti-Federalists, the two constituencies fought over who should get the credit for proposing the Second Amendment.

The founders' own writings illustrate that they considered the right to bear arms no less important than the other individual liberties guaranteed in the Constitution.

James Madison, the principal drafter of the Bill of Rights, recognized that all of these rights, including the right to bear arms, were "essential and sacred rights [that] *each individual* reserves to himself." Thomas Jefferson, the principal drafter of the Declaration of Independence, lumped all of these "human rights" together: "*[T]he people* . . . [have] the right and duty at all times to be armed; that they are entitled to freedom of person, freedom of religion, freedom of property, and freedom of the press." And

Tench Coxe, a Federalist advocating that Americans would not lose their right to arms under the new Constitution, wrote, "Their swords, and every other terrible implement of the soldier, are *the birth right* of an American . . . [under the Constitution] the unlimited power of the sword is not in the hands of either the federal or state governments, but where I trust in God it will ever remain, *in the hands of the people*" (my emphases).

Generations after the Founding Fathers had passed on, the Second Amendment remained a guarantee of an individual right. Duke Law School Professor William Van Alstyne sarcastically noted that, for the absurd "collective right" theory to be true, it must be "one of the most closely guarded secrets of the eighteenth century" since it is found in "no known writing from the period between 1787 and 1791." And another scholar, Professor David B. Kopel, wrote a 183-page analysis of every single nineteenth-century reference to the Second Amendment; not a single reference suggested the "collective right" theory. Did James Madison really dupe America into a conspiracy theory that tops the quest to determine how John F. Kennedy was assassinated?

NO GUNS FOR YOU

As described earlier, gun control in the twentieth century developed largely as a means of tyrannical social control. Government officials justified their assault on the right to self-defense by claiming that the Second Amendment was "outdated" and "useless." And these legislators, with the help of liberal judges, developed their fallacious "collective right" legal theory in order to entrench themselves in perpetual tyranny over the American people.

In the Clinton administration, overzealous gun-control advocates sought to reduce violence by taking guns away from law-abiding inner-city blacks.

Because such a law smacks of racism, they proposed something slightly more circuitous: a national ban on all firearms in public housing projects. Couldn't Bill Clinton, a Rhodes Scholar and graduate of Yale Law School, read the Second Amendment and realize that neither he nor Congress had the authority to strip law-abiding individuals of their constitutional guarantee of self-defense, especially where it was most desperately needed?

While efforts to enact a national ban ultimately failed, many states passed laws that similarly strip individuals in public housing of their right to keep and bear arms. What inevitably happens in these housing projects is that the law-abiding individuals surrender their arms while *criminals* refuse to comply with the firearm ban. Once the law-abiding individuals are disarmed, crime rises because it becomes significantly easier for gang members possessing the illegal guns to terrorize the law-abiding individuals who are unable to defend themselves.

The old saying, "when guns are outlawed, only outlaws will have guns," never rang truer than in a public housing project.

But the Clinton administration was hardly put off. To further facilitate the disarmament of law-abiding individuals, the misguided Clinton administration coupled gun buyback programs to these local public housing firearms bans. Thinking it could induce people into turning over their arms, the government would pay an individual about fifty dollars for each gun handed over (regardless of its condition).

Did the government really believe that criminals would accept fifty bucks for their illegal firearms? Sadly, yes. But, worse, the buyback programs quickly devolved into a scam. Criminals stole or cheaply purchased non-working handguns, collected fifty dollars from the government, and used the proceeds to buy more illegal handguns. Of course, some elderly citizens—not exactly a demographic that commits violent crimes—were induced to turn over their weapons so that they could have the extra cash. Essentially, American taxpayers spent fifteen million for some broken guns.

The government likes to ignore the reality that violence is increased when only the criminals are armed, telling people that the police are there to protect them. Yet, since public housing projects are so dangerous, many metropolitan police departments have established procedures whereby a police officer must wait for backup before he enters the housing project. If the police ever arrive, they are generally too late to stop the crime. The Founding Fathers, never imagining public housing but recognizing that law enforcement may not arrive at the scene of the crime until it is too late, established the Second Amendment to avoid this exact situation, in which an individual is rendered defenseless and unable to repel an intruder until the police arrive.

WHEN SELF-DEFENSE IS A CRIME

When individuals assert their fundamental human right of self-defense, government officials are often outraged; a tyrannical government is not happy with the power to employ violence in the hands of the people, rather than monopolized in the hands of the government.

Ronald Dixon, a Jamaican immigrant and a U.S. Navy veteran, legally purchased a gun in Florida and was in the process of registering it in Brooklyn, New York, where he lives. On the night of December 14, 2002, Dixon was awakened by sounds of a burglar in his home. He saw an intruder enter the bedroom of his two-year-old son. He used his gun to fire two shots into the intruder's chest. The intruder, Ivan Thompson, had five previous felony convictions; his fourteen-page rap sheet included numerous instances of burglary and larceny.

Dixon did nothing more than exercise his natural right to protect his family against a vile human being who meant them harm, yet Brooklyn District Attorney Charles Hynes decided to make him into a criminal. Dixon faced a penalty of up to one year imprisonment, after being arrested for illegally possessing a handgun. Hynes, displaying logic that would outrage even a first-grader, proclaimed, "We're not disputing that Mr. Dixon had a right to shoot the person who broke into his house. But he had no right to have that gun."

What was he to shoot the invader with, Mr. Hynes? Did Hynes expect

Dixon to watch the intruder murder his two-year-old and pray that the police show up in time? Or should Dixon have called Hynes to expedite his gun registration before he pulled the trigger?

Who in their right mind would not use a gun under these circumstances to save an innocent, defenseless baby?

After national outrage among members of the media and supporters of the Second Amendment, led by my Fox News colleague Sean Hannity, Hynes agreed to let Dixon escape jail time by pleading guilty to a "disorderly conduct" violation. Even though Dixon never went to jail, the State of New York clearly violated his Second Amendment rights. His life never should have been disrupted by the district attorney, he never should have been threatened with imprisonment for exercising a natural right, and he should not have had to incur legal expenses.

Dixon's tragedy is closer to the rule rather than the exception. Hale DeMar, a restaurant owner who lives in the suburban village of Wilmette, Illinois, with his wife and children, was burglarized on two consecutive nights. Morio Billings, who was convicted of a home burglary in 2002, entered DeMar's home on December 29, 2003, by crawling through the "dog door" in the garage. That night, he stole the keys to DeMar's house; he also stole the keys to DeMar's SUV and drove away in the vehicle. The following night, Billings returned to DeMar's home and entered with the stolen house keys. DeMar heroically confronted Billings in the kitchen and shot Billings in the shoulder and calf.

Of course, the episode did not end with Billings being sent to jail. DeMar was arrested on two criminal counts, and faced up to a year in jail. The top charge against DeMar was for owning a handgun without a valid firearms card. DeMar purchased his gun legally and registered it. His only "crime" was failing to renew his Illinois Firearm Owner's Identification Card when it expired. Since when is the Second Amendment—which guarantees *all* law-abiding individuals the right to self-defense—open for repeal by local prosecutors?

Wilmette Police Chief George Carpenter, who misguidedly went after

DeMar, turned a blind eye to the reality of the situation. He announced that "Wilmette residents are much safer without a handgun in their homes."

Can Carpenter say with a straight face that DeMar would have been safer if he were defenseless in the face of the burglary? Why was Billings, who had been convicted of burglarizing another home within the previous year, even on the streets?

Rather than commending DeMar for properly handling the situation, Carpenter stated that "for the safety of the home . . . a resident who finds himself in this situation [should] immediately lock the door of the room he's in and dial 911." Much good a cheap room door lock would have done; the Second Amendment means that you do *not* have to put a lock on the door of your bedroom and hide under your bed until the police arrive. After public outrage, the charges against DeMar were eventually dropped.

LEGAL YES, LEGAL NO

The federal government may strip you of your Second Amendment rights, even before you have the opportunity to defend yourself against a violent crime.

Timothy Joe Emerson, a law-abiding Texas physician, was indicted by a federal grand jury on the mere basis of possessing a firearm that he *lawfully owned*. When his wife filed for divorce in 1997, the divorce court judge routinely imposed twenty-nine restraining orders against Dr. Emerson. One of these orders prohibited him from threatening or injuring his wife; the judge made no findings and heard no evidence suggesting that Dr. Emerson had ever done so or that he was likely to do so in the future. This type of restraining order is routinely entered in contested divorce cases in certain states. Dr. Emerson had no opportunity to appeal this order.

Since Dr. Emerson was subject to that restraining order, it became a federal crime under the 1994 Violent Crime Control Act (commonly referred to as the "assault weapons ban") for Emerson legally to possess a firearm.

Under this statute, an individual is *automatically* stripped of his Second Amendment rights if a divorce court issues an order preventing that individual from using or threatening to use physical force against a family member, even if that individual's behavior is completely lawful. Further, Dr. Emerson's lack of knowledge of this obscure law and lack of intent to break it did not preclude his conviction.

Essentially, because the divorce court told Dr. Emerson to obey the law, the federal government swooped in and invoked an obscure federal law in order to deprive him of his constitutional right to keep and bear arms. Only in present-day America can it be illegal to perform a legal act.

In a major victory for individual liberty, Judge Sam Cummings, a U.S. District Judge in Texas, ruled that the indictment against Dr. Emerson was unconstitutional. Previously, no federal judge had ever declared a gun control statute to violate the Second Amendment. Judge Cummings wrote that prohibiting Emerson from owning a gun because he *might* threaten someone is similar to prohibiting an individual from ever opening his mouth because he might commit libel at some point in his life.

Unfortunately, the U.S. Court of Appeals for the Fifth Circuit reversed Judge Cummings' ruling and reinstated the indictment against Dr. Emerson, since the Second Amendment has always been "subject to . . . limited, narrowly tailored exceptions or restrictions." Appeals Court Judge William Garwood ducked having to declare the federal statute unconstitutional, writing that Congress was within its power to deprive an individual of his Second Amendment rights when he is subject to such a restraining order.

While this outcome is a disappointment for Dr. Emerson and for the rights guaranteed by the Second Amendment, the rationale behind it stands as a phenomenal victory for the Second Amendment. Judge Garwood turned to an "analysis of history and wording of the Second

Amendment for guidance," and reaffirmed the intentions of James Madison and Thomas Jefferson. Finding nothing in two hundred years of Supreme Court precedent to justify the "collective right" theory, the Court "reject[ed] the collective rights . . . model . . . for interpreting the Second Amendment." Judge Garwood powerfully stated that the Second Amendment "protects the right of *individuals*, including those not then actually a member of any militia or engaged in active military service or training, to privately possess and bear their own firearms" (my emphasis).

SUPREME DISAPPOINTMENT

While the Fifth Circuit has reaffirmed the Second Amendment's guarantee of an individual's right to keep and bear arms, every other U.S. Court of Appeals that has addressed this has managed to rule the other way. Yet, the U.S. Supreme Court once again declined to hear the case and resolve this split among circuits.

What is the Supreme Court afraid of, in declining to hear every single Second Amendment case that has come before it since 1939? It is time for the judiciary to abide by its constitutional duty to act as the final arbiter of individual rights, including the basic human right to self-defense.

Constitutional chaos and loss of innocent life: That's what happens when the government violates the Constitution. Just think what might have been avoided if law-abiding Americans had been armed on those ill-fated planes on September 11th 2001.

5

FILCHING PROPERTY

The right to private property is fundamental to freedom and individual liberty. However, there are rare instances when it is practical for the government to acquire private property for the general public's use. When the government acquires an individual's private property, it is considered a "taking." The source of the government's right to take private property is the "despotic power" or the "eminent domain power."

The traditional uses of the government's eminent domain power include public uses such as building roads, constructing schools, and saving wildlife. Historians have traced this legitimate use of governmental power back to ancient times.

The Romans, who constructed straight roads from one end of the empire to the other, used the power of eminent domain to confiscate land on which to build the roads. The aqueducts were erected under similar circumstances. However, the concept of compensating the victims of these confiscations was foreign to the Romans.

TAKINGS AND THE CONSTITUTION

America's Founding Fathers, even with their strong commitment to private property rights, recognized it was necessary for the government to have some eminent domain power. However, they also correctly recognized that the eminent domain power was subject to much governmental abuse and corruption. Human and economic nature provide the government with an *incentive* to abuse this power.

Left unchecked, the government can simply condemn your property and give it to a favored developer (who contributes to a mayor or governor's reelection campaign). And the developers do not have to negotiate with you to pay a fair price for your property. Only *you* lose, and how can you complain to the corrupt government that confiscated your land in the first place?

The government's eminent domain power is recognized in the Takings Clause (or the Just Compensation Clause), which is found in the Fifth Amendment to the U.S. Constitution. That clause states, "[N]or shall private property be taken for public use, without just compensation."

This clause is not a positive grant of power to the government. Rather, it places a *limitation* on governmental power, since the Constitution protects the rights of individuals and limits the powers of the government. The Constitution and the Declaration of Independence make clear that the government's only legitimate power is to secure the rights that are guaranteed to the people. As James Madison said, "As a man is said to have a right to his property, he may be equally said to have property in his rights." Therefore, the Constitution expresses the extremely limited power of the government to condemn private property.

The two pertinent phrases of the Takings Clause are "just compensation" and "public use." The "just compensation" requirement ensures that the government fairly compensates the victim of the taking. The victim must be "made whole," meaning that he is economically no worse off as a result of the taking. The government is forbidden from showing up at your door and taking title to your house, unless it pays you fair market value. It must also pay for your moving expenses, and losses that you incur while establishing yourself elsewhere.

The "public use" requirement, combined with the just compensation requirement, serves to limit further the government's eminent domain power. This requirement ensures that the taking is legitimate. The government has no right to condemn your property and give it to your neighbor, no matter how much it chooses to compensate you. Accordingly, the government has no authority to take your property—under any circumstances—for a private use.

The Constitution's framers saw first-hand the extent to which a government could abuse private property rights through its eminent domain power. In drafting the Takings Clause, the framers sought to ensure that the U.S. government would not operate as the King of England did.

The King asserted that his eminent domain power included dominion of the sea, control over navigation, defense of the realm, and even providing for *his household*. Frequently, the King would use or take private land—or even destroy it—without providing any compensation whatsoever. In 1606, the King decided to take private land in order to dig for saltpeter, without paying the owners of the land. The rationalization was that the saltpeter was used for gunpowder to defend the realm. Similarly, the King would often order fortification structures to be built on private land. The King even had the power to take someone's land so that his advisors could live on it!

The King also had broad latitude to abuse the eminent domain power in the colonies, since public roads needed to be built throughout the vast, unexplored continent. While the King did compensate landowners of developed or "improved" property, those who held title to unimproved property received no compensation. Even when the King paid compensation, it was a diminutive sum of money rather than the property's full value.

As the Constitution states, the government may only use its eminent domain power to take private property for a "public use." In the eighteenth and nineteenth centuries, the definition of a "public use" was exactly what it seems to mean: a use by the public. Over the last hundred years, however, corrupt and power-hungry government officials, combined with sympathizing courts, have completely transformed and perverted the Takings Clause.

Today, "public use" means "public benefit," and a "public benefit" can be a *private use,* whereby the government and its developer-friends claim that it "benefits" the public. When did Congress and thirty-eight states amend the Constitution to change the Takings Clause from "public use" to "private use"?

PUBLIC USE

In America, the nineteenth century saw vast territorial expansion, industrialization, and urbanization. As a result, the government frequently needed to use the eminent domain power to provide new services to the public.

During this period, the government actually followed the Constitution and used its power for only public uses, such as railroads, canals, and highways. In 1888 the New York Court of Appeals (the state's highest court) found constitutional the government's use of eminent domain to acquire land to build a privately owned railroad. The court noted, "The duty of providing public ways is . . . a public duty" because "railroads are highways furnishing means of communication between different points, promoting traffic and commerce, facilitating exchanges." The court stated that it was irrelevant that the public use was being carried out by a private corporation, because a for-profit railroad can provide services to the public more efficiently and economically than the government can.

Public uses of the government's eminent domain power were also found in water rights cases. The New York Court of Appeals ruled it constitutional for the government to condemn land so that a private company could build a dam to create reservoirs to provide water to certain specified towns. Even though the reservoirs benefited individuals only in select towns, the public use was still "in common and not for a particular individual."

PRIVATE GAIN

The previous examples demonstrate the proper function of eminent domain—the government's taking of land for *use* by the public. The radical transformation of the Takings Clause to mean "public benefit" rather than "public use" began in the early twentieth century. A landmark 1936 New York Court of Appeals case, *New York City Housing Authority v. Muller*, was the beginning of the end of private property rights in America.

That court determined "slum clearance" to be a public use. The New York City Housing Authority sought to acquire land to build a low-income housing project, so it used its eminent domain power to take title to two slum tenement buildings. But the housing project is not, by any circumstances, a *public use*. While the entire public can use land that is taken for construction of a railroad or a water reservoir, the housing project was not for public use and could only be used by the few individuals who resided there. This is a quintessential private use: the government took land from private individuals so that other private individuals could use that land to live on.

The court illogically concluded that this sort of private use was really a public use because it benefited the public. The State of New York asserted that the tenements were unsanitary, overcrowded, and substandard; they caused juvenile delinquency, crime, immorality, and economic loss to the state. The court stated that the elimination of this slum area was a "public purpose," and that it was constitutionally sufficient that the public *benefited* from this taking of private land.

Blatantly ignoring the fact that the Constitution uses the phrase "public use" rather than "public benefit," the court concluded, "The law of each age is ultimately what that age thinks should be the law." So, if the government decides to undergo a sociological experiment by clearing out a slum, it can violate the Constitution by stripping a private citizen of his land so that another private citizen can use his land.

Once "slum clearance" was established as a constitutionally acceptable means of perverting the Takings Clause, governments began using "slum clearance" as a front for violating private property rights to acquire land for their pet projects.

In the 1953 case of *Kaskel v. Impellitteri*, the New York Court of Appeals approved the government's use of the eminent domain power to condemn 6.3 acres of private land in order to build a "Coliseum" on Manhattan's Columbus Circle. The government's argument—that the Coliseum was a slum clearance project—was a sham: Judge Van Voorhis' dissent indicates that the government was "under the power of eminent domain, acquiring title from one private owner and transferring it to another without substantial reason."

Shockingly, only 2 percent of the condemned land was in fact a slum! Only 27.1 percent of the site was occupied for dwelling purposes. In fact, 39.1 percent of the site area was occupied by valuable business and commercial buildings. As Judge Van Voorhis stated, any slum clearance was "merely incidental."

Clearly, this project had nothing to do with slum clearance. The government simply wanted a large arena to be erected. The court's majority ruled that it was constitutionally sufficient that *the government* stated that the Coliseum was a slum clearance project. Aren't the courts supposed to monitor a corrupt government? How could they have ignored the fact that 98 percent of the land was not a slum? Nothing stops the government from condemning six more acres of private land—which happens to include a small slum area—for another pet project that clearly isn't a "public use." If courts simply took the government at its word, government officials would eventually find a way to condemn all of the private land they coveted. With the help of an inattentive court, the government blatantly violated the Constitution's Takings Clause. The Coliseum was sold to private developers who in 2002 razed it and built a luxury hotel in its place.

The government's perversion of "public use" didn't stop at slum clearance. In the 1940 case of *Bush Terminal Co. v. City of New York*, the New York Court of Appeals again refused to stop the government from condemning private land so that a private corporation could erect a sixteen-story commercial building to rent manufacturing and office space to the public for a profit.

The basement and a portion of the first story of this building were used to handle the delivery of freight and cargo into the Port of New York. The court rationalized this constitutional breach by finding that the private use of land for freight delivery economically benefited the public by allowing goods to come into the city. But the Constitution prohibits the government from using its eminent domain power for a private use, no matter how much the government claims that the public will benefit from that private use.

Additionally, the court conceded that the rest of the building was a private use that didn't even have a public benefit! It dismissed this fact by stating that the commercial rental space was incidental to the freight terminal. How could fifteen and a half stories of a sixteen-story building possibly be incidental? It is as if the government and the courts decide to turn a blind eye to the plain language of the Constitution.

Having condemned private land after convincing a court that one-half of a floor of a sixteen-story building benefited the public, twenty-three years later the government condemned an entire thirteen-block area. In 1963, the government engaged in a land-grab in order to clear a thirteen-block tract of downtown Manhattan so that a private company could erect the World Trade Center complex. It condemned all of the private land in that neighborhood, including a mom-and-pop store called the Courtesy Sandwich Shop.

In the case of *Courtesy Sandwich Shop v. Port of New York Authority*, the Court of Appeals approved the government's egregious violation of constitutionally protected property rights based on the government's assertion that the complex to be built would generate additional tax revenue. In a powerful dissent, Judge Van Voorhis noted that eminent domain is limited to public *uses* because it is not sufficient "that a project may be desirable or that it may have some indirect public benefit." He correctly noted that the Constitution couldn't possibly have allowed the government to condemn property any time it helps the public good, because almost any taking will have "some nexus with the public good."

The government's erosion of public use, in favor of public benefit, is a hallmark of "collectivism" and "socialization" in the eyes of Judge Van Voorhis. The judge warned that the courts have a responsibility not to "disregard . . . the constitutional protection of private property and the stigmatization of the small . . . entrepreneur as standing in the way of progress." Furthermore, Judge Van Voorhis argued that claiming a "purpose to be public merely [because the government says so] passe[s] the point of no return of . . . diminishing . . . private capital [and] progressively . . . displac[ing] [it with] public capital." James Madison and the Founding Fathers would be spinning in their graves at this "destruction of the constitutional bases of private ownership and enterprise."

The final blow to "public use" was a 1954 U.S. Supreme Court case, *Berman v. Parker*. When the federal government condemned a mom-and-pop grocery store so that a private company could redevelop the land, the Supreme Court wrote Congress and state legislatures a blank check to use and abuse eminent domain. The court stated that it would simply look the other way even when there is no public use, since "the role of the judiciary in determining whether that power is being exercised for a public purpose is an extremely narrow one" and "the means of executing the project are for Congress and Congress alone to determine."

In recent years, since the courts have crippled the Constitution's "public use" requirement, governments have arrogantly misused their blank check power to condemn private property. One of the worst horror stories of the government's usurpation of private property rights can be found in the Detroit suburb of Poletown, Michigan. The case of *Poletown Neighborhood Council v. City of Detroit*, decided by the Supreme Court of Michigan in 1981, allowed the government to destroy a community so that General Motors could build an assembly plant. The government condemned a 465-acre community, which wasn't anything close to a slum, so that one of the nation's wealthiest corporations could increase its profit margin.

As a result of the new GM plant, 3,468 people were displaced and had their homes confiscated by the government. The court simply rubber-stamped the government's claim that the condemnation would benefit the public because the GM plant would result in the creation of six thousand new jobs.

The Constitution's public use requirement was intended to protect against just this sort of usurpation. If GM wanted the property, it should have been required to purchase it. The government's use of the eminent domain power to transfer private land from one private party to another is an unconstitutional private use, even if it creates one million new jobs. No "public benefit" can counterbalance the fact that 3,468 people lost their homes so that a wealthy company could become wealthier.

TRUMPING PRIVATE PROPERTY

Outrageous governmental abuse of the eminent domain power does not stop in Poletown, Michigan. In 1994, real estate mogul Donald Trump sought to expand the Trump Plaza Hotel and Casino in Atlantic City, New Jersey. Trump's plans included using Vera Coking's home of thirty-six years as a limousine waiting area. Trump made low-ball offers to Coking, who refused to sell her property. Trump proceeded to convince the New Jersey Casino Reinvestment Development Authority (CRDA) to condemn the property and sell it to him at well below market rates.

Shortly thereafter, Ms. Coking received the following notice in her mailbox: "You may be required to move within 90 days after you receive this notice. If you remain in possession of the property after that time, CRDA may be able to have you and your belongings removed by the sheriff." Not only did the CDRA rubber-stamp this unconstitutional use of the eminent domain power, but so did the Appellate Division of the Superior Court of New Jersey.

In 1998, the New Jersey Supreme Court came to Ms. Coking's rescue and found that the government had abused the Takings Clause of the New Jersey Constitution by taking an individual's private property for a billionaire's private use. But that decision didn't remedy the fact that an old lady was forced by her own government to endure two years of litigation to combat the significant yet illegitimate threat of losing her home.

Turn to the small town of Hurst, Texas. In 2000, the town fathers threatened to condemn 127 homes so that its largest taxpayer, a real estate company, could build a larger parking lot for the town's mall. Because the victims of eminent domain never truly receive "just compensation" for their losses, the threat of endless litigation often coerces individuals to sell their property to the developer for significantly below market price. Accordingly, the developer doesn't even need to negotiate with the homeowner, knowing that the homeowner will receive even less from an eminent domain proceeding.

Most of the families were coerced into selling their property to the developer; just ten refused. Despite the fact that the government used the eminent domain power for a clearly private use, a Texas trial judge allowed the developer to demolish the homes even though the lawsuit wasn't over. The Prohs and the Duval families had each owned their homes for thirty years. Most shockingly, Leonard Prohs was forced to move while his wife was in the hospital with brain cancer; she died five days after the house was demolished.

Phyllis Duval's husband, also in the hospital with cancer at the time, died one month after the demolition. When the Constitution is so clearly disregarded, not even life and death can stop a corrupt government from abusing its eminent domain power.

And these examples are not isolated occurrences. On a daily basis, the government can be found plotting to violate the Constitution in order to take away your land.

A recent report by the Castle Coalition, a nonprofit organization formed by the Institute for Justice, chronicled 10,382 governmental attempts to condemn private property for the benefit of other private individuals in the last ten years. The report also found the abuses to be widespread, as these attempts occurred in forty-one of the fifty states.

ABRIDGING THE FIFTH, BUFFET-STYLE

In recent years, the government has developed an even stronger tool for seizing private property. Condemning private property via the eminent domain power, whether for public or private use, still requires the government to pay "just compensation." When it comes to "partial takings," the government and the Supreme Court completely ignore the Fifth Amendment's Takings Clause.

A "partial taking" occurs when the government passes a law that deprives individuals of the full use of their property rights. Unlike a condemnation or "full taking," the government is not acquiring title to the property. Rather, the government is regulating the property by limiting the owner's ability to use the property. Despite the fact that the owner still retains title to the property, the regulation nevertheless results in a financial loss. Accordingly, the government can, without taking title, regulate private property to the extent that it becomes almost worthless, and not pay a dime to the owner.

This principle—that the government can make your property almost worthless without compensating you—was articulated in a 1992 Supreme Court case, *Lucas v. South Carolina Coastal Council.* In 1986, David Lucas paid $975,000 for two beachfront residential lots in a residential development on the Isle of Palms, a barrier island near Charleston, South Carolina. He intended to erect single-family residences on the lots, just as his neighbors on the immediately adjacent parcels had already done.

Less than two years after Lucas bought the property, the government deemed his property a "critical area" that needed to be protected from coastal erosion. As a result, Lucas was prohibited from building any improvements on the lots. Essentially, the government told Lucas, "It is too bad that you paid almost one million dollars for the land, but you're stuck with these empty lots." A spineless Supreme Court of South Carolina ruled this perfectly acceptable, since the government *said* that regulation was designed "to prevent a serious public harm."

The U.S. Supreme Court stepped in and gave a minor procedural victory to Lucas, while all but destroying private property rights. Justice Scalia, writing for the Court, ruled that Lucas was only entitled to compensation under the Takings Clause if the government's regulation had rendered his property "valueless."

Justice Scalia made an illogical bright-line distinction between a total taking and a partial taking. He reasoned that a regulation that deprives the owner of "all economically beneficial uses" (a total taking) requires just compensation, because it is equivalent to the government condemning the property and acquiring title. However, the property owner is entitled to *no compensation* for a partial taking, even if the regulation falls just short of making the properly "valueless."

In creating a worthless distinction between partial and total takings, the Supreme Court painted government a clear roadmap for invading private property rights while not compensating victims. In a nutshell, the court told government, "Don't take it all, and you don't have to pay anything."

Lucas's case was sent back to the South Carolina courts to determine whether the regulation made his property "valueless." It is hard to imagine *any* regulation that deprives an owner of *all* "economically beneficial uses" of his land; surely Lucas' beachfront property has *some* "value" even if he cannot build a house on it. Basically, the Court stated that Takings

Clause is meaningless if the government doesn't actually acquire title to the owner's land.

WETLANDS RIP-OFF

The 2001 Supreme Court case of *Palazzolo v. Rhode Island* illustrates the absurdity of the *Lucas* rule. In 1959, Anthony Palazzolo acquired a waterfront parcel of land in Westerly, Rhode Island. In 1971, the government decreed his property to be "protected coastal wetlands," meaning that he could only build on the property if he convinced the government that the activity served "a compelling public purpose which provides benefits to the public as a whole." Since when does private property need to provide benefits to the public? From 1983 to 1985, the government thrice rejected Palazzolo's proposals (a beach club and two different residential subdivisions) to develop his land.

Because the wetlands regulation essentially barred him from doing anything with the land, appraisers determined that Palazzolo's property was worth $200,000 rather than $3,150,000. The government's regulation, therefore, deprived him of 93.6 percent of his property's value.

Palazzolo sued the government, asking for "just compensation," on the grounds that the wetlands regulation amounted to an unconstitutional taking. The Supreme Court ruled that Palazzolo was not entitled to any compensation because he "failed to establish a deprivation of all economic value," since he was left with more than a "token interest."

The Supreme Court's arbitrary decision to ignore partial takings is ludicrous. Palazzolo was left with 6.4 percent of his property's value. For the Court to leave him with no remedy because the property isn't "valueless" is a perversion of the Takings Clause. Why should the government be able to deprive Palazzolo of $3 million of value and not pay him a dime, while the government would be required to pay full compensation when it condemns and acquires title to another landowner's $3 million property? Why didn't the government condemn Palazzolo's land if it so wished to protect the wetlands? The answer is simple: The government didn't want to pay anything, not even a dime, to Palazzolo. And it got away with it.

STICKY FINGERS

Sometimes government agents literally take property for *their* own use. I was once involved in a case concerning a young man whose eighty-five-thousand-dollar Mercedes-Benz roadster had been confiscated by the cops as evidence of a crime. The fellow had been arrested for using this sporty vehicle to transport women across the George Washington Bridge for illicit purposes.

The driver and his father later made an application for return of the Benz. The cops had taken the car as evidence of a crime but had given it to the chief county prosecutor, who began driving it for his own *personal* use. I was the judge to whom the application to return the car was assigned. Since they hadn't charged the driver with anything and probably never intended to, and they just wanted to steal his property so he couldn't use it, I ordered the car to be returned.

About ten years later, I happened to be in a restaurant where I ran into this now-former prosecutor. He introduced me to his wife, who looked at me and then back to her husband and said, "Is this the judge who took your car away?"

6

GAGGING FREE SPEECH

The First Amendment explicitly prohibits the government from interfering with free speech. The Amendment is in danger—and its danger comes from the least likely of sources: the judiciary.

Every school child can recite: "Congress shall make no law . . . abridging the freedom of speech." But over the last few years, freedom of speech, the quintessential American liberty, has come under fire from several troubling rulings in which judges—the traditional defenders of individual liberties against the censoring potential of the government—have abused their authority to restrict the content of speech in a frightening manner.

THE RECENT ASSAULT

In 1999, a federal jury in Oregon punished the authors of a Web site with a one-hundred-million-dollar fine for their provocative anti-abortion writings. The year before, the United States Supreme Court let stand a federal judge's bizarre perpetual gag order forbidding former jurors from speaking to the media—ever—about their deliberations, absent special permission from the judge herself.

A Greenville, Mississippi, newspaper reporter was arrested and incarcerated for criminal contempt for publishing a criminal defendant's juvenile record even though it was read aloud in an open courtroom during sentencing. In 1997, a Wilmington, North Carolina, newspaper was fined more than five hundred thousand dollars for publishing truthful details of a secret settlement agreement in an environmental pollution case, although the reporter received the information directly from the court clerk.

The federal judge handling the Oklahoma City bombing case enforced a gag order forbidding federal prosecutors from communicating with state prosecutors for months beyond the conclusion of the trial. And in a first for pop music, in the traditional civil liberties stronghold of Northern California, an up-and-coming rap music artist was arrested and jailed for mouthing angry political lyrics that were unkind to the traditional target of youth-oriented music: the police.

In an unbroken string of First Amendment rulings in the past three decades, the United States Supreme Court has declared that expressive liberties may not be interfered with by the government absent a very strong governmental justification—such as protecting a real and present threat to national security—for doing so.

Whether it is the right of Amish parents to promote their religion by educating young adults at home rather than in high school or the right of the press to publish the name of a juvenile offender or a rape victim when the press has lawfully obtained the information, the court has steadfastly protected our First Amendment rights by placing a heavy onus on the government to justify the desired intrusion on the content of individual expressive liberties.

Yet recent cases demonstrate a waning commitment by our courts to act as the protectors of speech liberties guaranteed by the First Amendment. Why is the fundamental right to free speech overlooked when a parole officer decides to have a rap artist arrested because the officer disapproves of what the singer is saying? Where is the strong protection owed to the press when blameless news reporters are arrested and fined for publishing the truth merely because a judge objects? Can the government override the fundamental right to free speech when a judge denies jurors the right to speak about their experiences, cuts off the media's access to jurors willing to speak, or forbids communication among prosecutors long after the judge's control over the participants in the court system has terminated?

JUSTIFIABLE RESTRICTIONS

While courts more frequently tell us what governmental interests do *not* qualify as a basis for interfering with the content of speech rather than what interests *do*, the Supreme Court has indicated that certain governmental interests may be of such a magnitude that suppression of the First Amendment's guarantee of a free press may be justified. In so doing, however, the court pointed to just one such example of a government interest of the highest order: national security in times of war.

Citing the Depression-era case of *Near v. Minnesota*, in which the court hypothesized that "publication of the sailing dates of transports or the number and location of troops" during wartime could constitutionally be blocked, notwithstanding the First Amendment, Justice Thurgood Marshall suggested that only those governmental interests that speak to the *continued existence of the government itself* rise to the constitutional level sufficient to override expressive liberties.

It is difficult to imagine a government interest greater than preserving national security during wartime, thereby preserving the existence of the state itself, and it is telling indeed that Justice Marshall cited no other example of a governmental interest of significant magnitude (known as a "state interest of the highest order") to override expressive liberties.

BUT WHEN IS A GAG TOO BIG?

In two opinions written recently by Chief Justice Rehnquist, the Supreme Court put the government to the test of demonstrating a need to further a very strong governmental justification and a means narrowly tailored toward advancing that interest before the government could justify impairment of the *content* of the free speech of an individual.

In one of these cases, *United States v. Aguilar*, the Supreme Court reviewed the conviction of a federal judge for illegally disclosing the existence of an FBI wiretap and for obstruction of justice for lying to federal agents investigating an embezzlement conviction.

The court acknowledged that "the government may not generally restrict individuals from disclosing information that lawfully comes into their hands" unless the government has a very important and compelling justification. But Chief Justice Rehnquist noted that the wiretap statute does not broadly sanction all those who disclose lawfully obtained knowledge of a wiretap, but is sufficiently narrowly tailored such that it imposes liability "only on those who disclose wiretap information 'in order to obstruct, impede, or prevent'" interception of the communications that are the focus of the probe.

Beyond this narrow impingement on speech, Chief Justice Rehnquist reasoned that the government may at times impose "special duties of nondisclosure" upon "officials in sensitive confidential positions," like federal judges, such that an impairment of a judge's First Amendment rights is justified even where it would not be so for the rights of "a member of the general public who happened to lawfully acquire possession of information about a wiretap."

Citing the need to "preserve the integrity of the court" and justifying the higher duty imposed on government officials who voluntarily assumed a position of confidentiality, Chief Justice Rehnquist concluded that "the Government's interest" in maintaining the secrecy of sensitive wiretap information "is quite sufficient to justify" application of the statute to a federal judge "without any artificial narrowing because of First Amendment concerns."

In another opinion written by Chief Justice Rehnquist in this vein, *Butterworth v. Smith*, the Supreme Court considered the First Amendment rights of a former grand jury witness to speak about the subject matter of the grand jury investigation after the completion of the proceedings. A Florida statute prohibited grand jury witnesses from *ever* disclosing their testimony, and one such witness sued to have the statute declared an unconstitutional impairment of his free speech rights as guaranteed by the First Amendment.

Chief Justice Rehnquist analyzed that claim and declared that a state may not sanction *the content* of an individual's speech regarding lawfully obtained truthful information, absent a very important governmental justification. Because the state was unable to demonstrate that its restriction on grand jury witnesses was narrowly tailored to advance a very important governmental justification (like protecting troops during wartime), the court struck down the statute insofar as it operated to bar indefinitely the communication of truthful information lawfully obtained by grand jury witnesses.

Requiring the government to have a very important justification— one which if not served presently would adversely affect the structural integrity of the state itself—for violating the right to free speech serves the needs of individuals and government because it not only endeavors to secure constitutional liberties but allows for an override in situations of the utmost state interest.

When an expressive liberty is impaired, the courts must put the state to the test to explain the necessity of infringing upon that individual liberty. Such a requirement is the quintessence of the Bill of Rights, which secures and defends the rights of individuals against the government. The onus properly belongs on the state when its actions have negative consequences for the exercise of expressive liberties.

FREE SPEECH, BUT WATCH YOUR MOUTH!

With free speech guaranteed by the Constitution and owed strong protection by the courts, how does one explain the $107 million punishment handed down by a federal district court against the purveyors of "The Nuremberg Files," an anti-abortion Web site, in a rebuke of the group's strident anti-abortion messages?

The verdict was premised on a theory that the inflammatory images and the content of the Web site provoked violence against abortion-providing physicians. The plaintiffs sued under a federal statute prohibiting violence that blocks access to abortion clinics. The defendants asserted a First Amendment defense, maintaining that their "Wanted" posters depicting abortion providers alongside graphic images, including fetuses dripping with blood, were constitutionally protected free speech. The jury, however, found that the Web site's information could reasonably be construed as a "true threat" of violence to abortion providers and thus fell within the "incitement to violence" exception to the First Amendment's sphere of protection.

In a case that has raised the ire of numerous journalists and media commentators, the U.S. Supreme Court refused to get involved in *In re Capital City and Joe Gyan*, thus allowing to stand the affirmation by the U.S. Court of Appeals for the Fifth Circuit of a federal judge's order that barred jurors from discussing their deliberations with the media even after the conclusion of the trial.

The order, issued by U.S. District Judge Sarah S. Vance, has the effect of forbidding—in perpetuity—the media from interviewing jurors regarding their deliberations absent a special order from the judge herself permitting the given questions to be asked. Upon completion of the criminal trial, Judge Vance directed the jurors that "absent a special order by me, no juror may be interviewed by anyone concerning the deliberations of the jury."

By declining to review the case, the Supreme Court has allowed federal trial courts in Louisiana, Mississippi, and Texas to impose restrictions on the speech rights of jurors and the media that are far more intrusive on expressive liberties, and with far less governmental justification, than would withstand scrutiny.

The gag order at issue begs the question of what order of magnitude a governmental interest must meet in order to justify silencing individual speakers and the media. One would not seriously dispute that the administration of justice is a compelling interest, yet it seems clear that there must be some moment when the magnitude of that interest dissipates: when the discussion of jury deliberations may not pose a "substantial threat" to the justice system. Judge Vance's order was *perpetual*. Absent an order granting permission from the judge herself, the jurors may *never* be interviewed regarding their deliberations.

Imposing a blanket gag order on the entire jury, restricting the speech rights of each juror as well as the public's right to know, and impairing the media's right to gather news about truthful issues of consuming public interest is certainly not the narrowest way to safeguard open, free speech in a jury room.

Court orders impairing media access to information regarding trials require consideration of the full panoply of alternatives before a restriction on speech may be applied. It is sheer judicial arrogance—even lunacy—to maintain that a judge can sit in judgment of what questions the media may ask, and indeed, what members of the media may interview a given witness, and that such a power can last *forever*, regardless of the remoteness of the trial.

Taking Judge Vance's order to its logical, though absurd, conclusion, a juror in a high-profile case can be prohibited *for life* from discussing her thoughts about the deliberations process. Even the posthumous publication of the juror's autobiography would violate the order unless the trial judge had herself approved the publication. There is no jurisprudential basis for this constitutional anomaly of a judge sitting as a super-editor-in-chief. Judge Vance's ruling is clearly at odds with cases that have determined that gag orders placed on jurors are not supported by sufficiently important governmental justifications for violating free speech.

GOING AFTER REPORTERS

In two very odd cases, trial judges meted out unduly harsh punishments against reporters and the newspapers for which they worked, merely because the judge preferred that the newspapers not exercise their First Amendment right to publish the information.

Greenville, Mississippi, reporter Cynthia Jeffries was arrested and held in criminal contempt for disobeying a judge's order not to publish a criminal defendant's juvenile record even though the defendant's record was read aloud in an open courtroom during his sentencing.

You cannot unring a bell; once data is in the public domain, anyone who heard or saw it can repeat it.

The contempt order against Jeffries was eventually dismissed, but only after the attorney general of Mississippi asked the state supreme court to dismiss the conviction on the grounds that the judge's order was unconstitutional and that the reporter was, therefore, correct to disobey it. If a reporter has to rely on the state's highest prosecutor to defend her constitutional liberties rather than on an independent judiciary, we have a constitutional anomaly rather than a reliable standard.

The Wilmington, North Carolina, *Morning Star* and its Raleigh bureau chief, Kirsten Mitchell, were not so fortunate as to have a freedom-friendly prosecutor come to their defense when a federal district judge fined them five hundred thousand dollars for publishing the details of a settlement reached in an environmental pollution case of consuming local interest.

The terms of the settlement agreement were intended to be kept confidential, but the court clerk gave the information to Mitchell in a case file which should not have contained the settlement terms. But when Mitchell and the *Morning Star* exercised their First Amendment right to publish this truthful information that was lawfully, even if erroneously, obtained by them, U.S. District Judge Earl Britt held them in contempt and issued fines topping half-a-million dollars.

Judge Britt was far out of line in even attempting to punish the media for publishing truthful information that it lawfully obtained from his court clerk, especially given the fact that *the government itself* had the power to prevent dissemination of the sensitive information simply by policing itself better. The fact that the fine was half-a-million dollars makes it all the more egregious.

A similar situation arose during the rape proceedings against basketball superstar Kobe Bryant. Over the course of a two-day closed door hearing in June 2004, Bryant's accuser testified about her sexual history. A week later, the court reporter, intending to email the transcript of that hearing to other court employees, accidentally emailed the sealed transcript to seven media organizations. That same afternoon, Colorado State Judge Terry Ruckriegle issued an order barring the media organizations from publishing the transcript; he threatened criminal contempt for any member of the media who violated the order.

Seeking to exercise their free speech right to publish information that they had lawfully obtained, seven media organizations that received the transcript petitioned the Colorado Supreme Court to challenge Judge Ruckriegle's order. The Colorado Supreme Court upheld the gag order by a four-to-three vote.

How can the media engage in open, robust speech regarding public issues when its speech may expose it to arrest or six-figure liabilities? Newspapers cannot constitutionally be punished for publishing truthful information they lawfully receive when the government does not have a very important national security justification for prohibiting them from doing so.

MORE COURTROOM DRAMA

In the Oklahoma City bombing case, U.S. District Judge Richard P. Matsch was widely hailed for ruling his courtroom with an iron first during the 1997 trials of Timothy McVeith and Terry Nichols, and for avoiding the media bedlam that characterized the O.J. Simpson trial of the year before.

But whereas some praised Judge Matsch as the "anti-Ito"—a reference to California Superior Court Judge Lance Ito who limply presided over the O.J. Simpson criminal trial—defenders of the First Amendment have lamented a growing trend toward silencing participants in high-profile trials and restricting to private quarters judicial proceedings that have traditionally been held in public courtrooms.

Among those frustrated by Judge Matsch's heavy-handed control over all participants in the case was, somewhat surprisingly, an Oklahoma district attorney, who repeatedly petitioned the U.S. District Court for the District of Colorado seeking termination of Judge Matsch's gag order so that federal prosecutors and investigators might assist state officials with a state grand jury investigation of the Oklahoma City bombing. Oklahoma officials had to wait *a year* from the June 1997 conclusion of the federal trial until Judge Matsch lifted his gag order on attorneys, and four more months until the U.S. Court of Appeals for the Tenth Circuit affirmed that order. Judge Matsch's orders had far more devastating implications for the media's right to report issues of public concern and the public's right to observe and comprehend judicial proceedings.

Judge Matsch was much praised as the antidote to Judge Ito, but at what price? He ruled his courtroom with an iron fist, but he trammeled the liberty of prosecutors, investigators, the state of Colorado, the media, and the public in doing so. Such overbroad restrictions on speech are not permitted under the First Amendment and would likely be found invalid.

HIP HOP DROP

And what to make of the constitutionally aberrant arrest of Shawn Thomas, a California rap artist who was jailed due to the controversial nature of his lyrics? Thomas, who performs under the name C-Bo, was taken from his home and confined in the Sacramento County Jail after California Corrections Department officials determined that the lyrics on his album, "Til My Casket Drops," advocate violence against police and promote "the gang lifestyle."

Among Thomas's allegedly incendiary lyrics was a song that railed against former California Governor Pete Wilson for signing the state's "three strikes, you're out" law, under which minor violations such as shoplifting can land a repeat offender in jail for fifty years to life. This egregious impairment of Thomas's freedom of speech was justified by state officials as necessary to enforce the conditions of Thomas's parole for an earlier minor weapons-related offense.

The government convicted Thomas for "discharging an illegal firearm" when he fired a gun into the air to quell a fight that emerged during the filming of a music video. As rash as his behavior may have been, the bullet from Thomas's gun did not strike anyone. Thomas's parole was subject to very highly suspect conditions that implicate central First Amendment interests: He was told that in return for staying out of jail, he could not promote violence against police officers, promote "the gang lifestyle," or "threaten" any public officials, or he would find himself incarcerated.

Thomas's parole conditions are constitutionally suspect because they are so vague and so clearly contradict First Amendment jurisprudence regarding the state's ability to interfere with the advocacy of illegal conduct only when the speech presents a danger of "imminent lawless action" and where there is insufficient time to rebut the speech and thereby avoid the danger.

Beyond the highly suspect nature of the terms the state placed on Thomas's parole, his subsequent punishment for voicing his opinions is an unforgivable assault on the First Amendment. While C-Bo's lyrics may be offensive to some ("You better swing batter, batter swing/'cause once you get your third felony fifty years you gotta bring/It's a deadly game of baseball, so when they try to pull you over/shoot 'em in the face y'all."), they are clearly constitutionally protected speech—particularly the most objectionable of his songs, which represents his political opposition to California's harsh "three strikes" law.

When such political speech and advocacy of resistance to unjust, or even just, laws result in the speaker being hauled from his home and thrust into jail, the First Amendment has been assaulted in a manner that should incite the indignation of all Americans regardless of their opinions of C-Bo's lyrics or rap music in general.

What interest is being served by his arrest that could not be better served by educating the public against gang activity in order to counteract C-Bo's incendiary lyrics? Are protecting the feelings and comforts of the police and discouraging gang activity sufficient governmental justifications for violating free speech, such that the state's continued existence would be at risk from a failure to sanction this rapper from rhyming in a way that suggests violence against the police? Can such an interest ever justify preventing a person from speaking his mind when there is time to rebut the offensive speech with more speech?

Speaking about violence is only punishable when it is an incitement to likely imminent lawlessness. As with the Nuremberg Files Web site, communication via a rap song that one listens to at home is certainly subject to ample time to rebut. Additionally, there are alternative means to serve the state's interest in combating Thomas's involvement with gang violence, such as restricting his parole so that he may not pursue actual involvement in and promotion of gang violence. Punishing the rap artist for what he *says* rather than what he *does* is judicial arrogance *non pariel*, is patently offensive to the First Amendment, and could never have come about had the court properly determined that the government's justification was not sufficiently important.

PLEADING THE FIRST

The First Amendment should be read to compel all those who exercise government power, including members of the judiciary, to require the government to demonstrate a profound justification before the content of free speech liberties can be impaired. Judges are expected to be vigilant in scrutinizing the proper limits of governmental authority, irrespective of how popular the government's behavior may be, and they should be loath to issue gag orders and other restrictions on the speech of persons brought before or watching them.

There are some bright spots on the constitutional horizon. For example, the South Carolina Supreme Court rebuked two trial judges who closed pretrial hearings in a high-profile criminal case for failing to explore less restrictive alternatives that would still protect the defendant's right to a fair trail before ordering the proceedings closed. The Rhode Island Supreme Court, as well, struck down a blanket policy that denied access to court records relating to child molestation cases even when any identifying information had already been purged from the records. That court rightly found such a broad ban on access to be in violation of the First Amendment-protected right of access to criminal proceedings because such a ban was not narrowly tailored and was too restrictive.

But the media should not be made to litigate for the privilege of exercising rights it indisputably possesses. Why should these cases have had to make it to their states' highest court before the media was able to vindicate the constitutional rights that were guaranteed through landmark cases decades ago? Why should the media or individual defendants have to bear the cost of litigating when the Constitution and the controlling case law are so clearly on their side?

All of these horrific examples of the government violating the First Amendment totally contradict clear U.S. Supreme Court precedent. The landmark case of *Florida Star v. B.J.F.*, decided in 1989, established the principle that the government generally violates the constitutional guarantee of free speech by suppressing "lawfully obtained truthful information." In that case, a newspaper reporter legally photocopied a police report from a police department's public press room and proceeded to publish the full name of a rape victim. After a Florida court fined the newspaper for violating a law that prohibits such a disclosure of the rape victim's full name, the U.S. Supreme Court ruled this punishment to be inconsistent with the First Amendment, especially since *the government itself* made the victim's name available. Subsequent Supreme Court cases have similarly held that the government can't strip citizens and the media of their right to free speech, yet local prosecutors and judges refuse to learn.

Bush administration Attorney General John Ashcroft doesn't seem to have much use for the First Amendment. As he testified to the Senate, "To those who pit Americans against immigrants, citizens against non-citizens, to those who scare peace-loving people with phantoms of lost liberty, my message is this: Your tactics only aid terrorists for they erode our national unity and diminish our resolve." And by April 2004, Attorney General Ashcroft's "phantoms" had led us to a point where free speech almost does not exist. When the American Civil Liberties Union filed a lawsuit against the federal government challenging a national security letter (a secret search warrant that an FBI agent writes for himself), the Justice Department persuaded the trial judge in the case to subject *the entire case file* to a gag order. The government argued that the gag order was justified on the ground that, under the USA PATRIOT Act, those served with national security letters are forbidden from *talking* about them. The logical conclusion is that a party served with a national security letter can't even discuss the situation with his *lawyer*.

Only after months of negotiations between the government and the ACLU was the complaint that the ACLU filed against the government authorized for release. The document was filled with black markings, and even part of the case's title—*[CENSORED] and ACLU v. Ashcroft*—was redacted. Americans outraged with this blatant usurpation of the First Amendment right to free speech share concerns that are far more than "phantoms of lost liberty."

The U.S. Supreme Court has granted strident protection to the media in a narrow category of cases where the government attempted to punish the publication of lawfully obtained truthful information. This means that the government may curtail the content of expressive liberties only when the interests that the government seeks to serve *must* be served at the peril of the *demise of the government itself* if they go unserved and only where the government's interest in self-preservation can be served by no other means. This test offers a consistent, unifying standard that puts the constitutionally mandated, appropriately burdensome onus of justifying state impairment of expressive liberties on the government.

The First Amendment, the crown jewel of our constitutional democracy, would have Americans enjoy the exercise of our expressive liberties in the certain knowledge that, barring a state interest of the highest order, the courts will always safeguard the exercise of our expressive liberties.

7

BRIBING WITNESSES, BUYING CONVICTIONS

The government cannot place itself above the law. When the government ment wishes to bring a suspected criminal to justice, it must do so within the bounds of the law. If the government must resort to lawbreaking in order to obtain its conviction, even the most noble end—ensuring that justice is served—does not justify the ignoble means because justice is not served when the government breaks the law.

In every state in the Union, in every commonwealth and territory, and under the laws written by Congress, the buying of testimony constitutes a felony. A witness who receives something of value for his testimony at a criminal trial is likely to be dishonest, disingenuous, and unreliable. As such, the purpose of laws criminalizing the buying of a witness is to ensure fairness during the criminal trial and to prevent against a corrupt judicial system. According to the federal statute, "Whoever . . . gives, offers, or promises *anything of value* to any person, for . . . testimony under oath . . . shall be fined . . . or imprisoned for [up to] two years, or both" (my emphasis).

Despite this clear prohibition against the buying of testimony, government attorneys around the nation, from small-town prosecutors to the Department of Justice and the attorney general himself, violate this law on a daily basis. These prosecutors regularly pay government witnesses for their testimony, either in the form of cash payments or the witness's freedom—i.e., receiving a reduced jail sentence after entering into a favorable plea bargain.

INGRAINED INJUSTICE

The U.S. Court of Appeals for the Tenth Circuit has noted that this behavior is an "historic practice . . . of our criminal justice system" and is an "ingrained aspect of American legal culture."

But the practice is illegal. Since the law applies to "whoever" pays a witness to testify at a criminal trial, there is no exception for government prosecutors. It is perfectly clear why a defense attorney can't bribe a witness to testify on his client's behalf: justice cannot be served when the person on the witness stand is being paid to say presumably whatever it takes to ensure that he receives his payment. This same principle applies to government prosecutors who offer prosecution witnesses something of value in exchange for their testimony. Since it is irrational to think that a witness bribed by the government somehow has more credibility than a witness bribed by the defense, the law makes it a crime for *anyone* to bribe a witness.

Every government prosecutor, just like every criminal defense lawyer, is sworn to uphold the Constitution and the law. The rules that govern the professional conduct of lawyers provide that "a lawyer shall not . . . offer an inducement to a witness that is prohibited by law." The rule further specifies the "the common law rule . . . that it is improper to pay an occurrence witness [as distinguished from a hired expert witness] any fee for testifying," governs all lawyers. Government prosecutors are not exempt from their obligation to operate within the bounds of the law. This constant abuse proliferates because the government—which controls the machinery of the criminal justice system—rarely charges *its own prosecutors* with violating a law that hinders its ability to put people in jail.

The law that makes it a crime for a prosecutor to buy a witness's testimony does not simply represent a fear that prosecutors are corrupt and self-interested bureaucrats. The law exists primarily because there is a general mistrust of the *witnesses* who receive the payments rather than the attorneys who make the payments. Accordingly, a government prosecutor still violates the law even when he has absolutely no intent to influence the witness's testimony. Thus, even a good-natured, honest, and selfless prosecutor—of which there are many in the United States—who offers a witness a reduced sentence in exchange for his testimony in order to see that justice will be served against a heinous defendant, is still guilty of violating the criminal law prohibiting the buying of witness testimony.

The law recognizes the simple reality that *any* witness—prosecution or defense—whose testimony was secured with something of value has been bribed and is thus untrustworthy. An attorney who bribes a witness is acting contrary to the interests of justice, regardless of his motive for bribing the witness.

The primary duty of a government prosecutor is to ensure "that justice shall be done," according to a 1935 U.S. Supreme Court case, *Berger v. United States*. Since the prosecutor is the "servant of the law" and a representative of a government "whose obligation [is] to govern impartially," it is improper for the prosecutor to break the law in order to win a case. According to Justice Sutherland, "He may prosecute with earnestness and vigor—indeed he should do so. But, while he may strike hard blows, he is not at liberty to strike foul ones. It is as much his duty to refrain from improper methods calculated to produce a wrongful conviction as it is to use every legitimate means to bring about a just one."

The law clearly recognizes the threat to the integrity of the justice system that occurs when a lawyer pays a witness to testify at a criminal trial and applies the prohibition against witness bribery to all attorneys, including prosecutors. As Justice Brandeis wrote in *Olmstead v. United States,* "[T]o declare that . . . the end justifies the means . . . would bring terrible retribution."

The current procedure for filtering out incredible witness testimony—allowing the defense attorney to cross-examine the government witness so that the jury hears that the testimony was secured with a bribe—is wholly inadequate. It is blantantly prejudicial and improperly influential for the jury even to *hear* what a bribed prosecution witness has to say, even if the defense has the ability to attack that witness's credibility by exposing the bribe.

Additionally, when a bribed prosecution witness takes the stand, it is the *jury's* prerogative to determine whether the witness is credible. Because that testimony is illegal, it is inherently unfair to the defendant, and to the judicial process, for the jury to be left to evaluate which bribed witnesses are and aren't credible.

The class of individuals who are most likely to receive payment for their testimony not only have the most incentive to commit perjury, but also make very credible and believable witnesses. This is so because the government often makes a deal with a "lesser" criminal—who rats out a "bigger" criminal—whose livelihood is based on his ability to lie and get away with it.

TESTIMONY ON THE AUCTION BLOCK

In 1992, the federal government indicted Sonya Singleton and Napoleon Douglas, along with dozens of others, on multiple counts of money laundering and conspiracy to distribute cocaine. Singleton was arrested in Wichita, Kansas, after law enforcement suspected that she helped wire drug money ("over $1000" according to the court) between Kansas and California. Douglas was the only person the government could find to identify Singleton as part of the conspiracy. For whatever reason, the federal prosecutors determined that they would rather go hard after Singleton and go easy on Douglas. Accordingly, in order to secure Douglas's testimony against Singleton, the government made a "deal" with Douglas.

Douglas was facing a sentence of fifteen years for the crimes under the indictment. Additionally, the federal government was preparing to charge

Douglas with additional violations of the Drug Abuse Prevention and Control Act arising out of his activities. So, the federal prosecutors offered him a deal he couldn't refuse—as long as he explicitly promised to testify against Singleton and implicate her in the conspiracy. In exchange for implicating Singleton, Douglas served *four* years in prison, concurrently with time he was already obligated to serve in Mississippi. The government basically gave a free pass to someone it had considered to be a major criminal as payment for his testimony under oath.

Singleton's attorney filed a motion to suppress Douglas's testimony, since it was clearly in violation of the federal statute that criminalizes the buying of testimony. It is undeniable that the government offered and Douglas received something "of value" in exchange for his testimony, since the government's leniency amounted to his freedom. The trial judge decided to ignore the plain and unambiguous anti-bribery law and issued a one sentence ruling: "This statute does not apply to the Government." The government's conspiracy case consisted solely of the testimony that it purchased from Douglas, and that testimony was enough for the jury to return a guilty verdict. Singleton was sentenced to almost four years in federal prison.

Singleton appealed to the U.S. Court of Appeals for the Tenth Circuit, and a three-judge panel unanimously ruled that Douglas's testimony should have been suppressed because "the statutes cannot justify the government's promises [to Douglas] in this case." Because the government's violation of the law was so egregious, the court reversed Singleton's conviction and ordered the federal government to give her a new trial, without Douglas's bribed testimony.

The court's opinion, written by Judge Paul Kelly Jr., debunked the government's ludicrous argument that the word "whoever" in the anti-bribery statute means everyone but the government. Since the statute applies to "whoever . . . gives, offers, or promises anything of value to any person, for . . . testimony under oath," the statute cannot be read to exclude the government's own lawyers. Judge Kelly noted that "one of the very oldest principles of our legal heritage is that the king is subject to the law," tracing the principle from the Magna Carta in 1215 to Supreme Court precedent over the last two hundred years.

Judge Kelly powerfully expressed the court's central holding, a novel holding for a federal appellate court: "The judicial process is tainted and justice cheapened when factual testimony is purchased, whether with leniency or money. Because prosecutors bear a weighty responsibility to do justice and observe the law in the course of a prosecution, it is particularly appropriate to apply the [anti-bribery statute] to their activities."

The government sought to have the court ignore its lawbreaking on the basis that the government serves the interests of society—the greater good, it argued—by offering leniency to lesser criminals who make the case against more important defendants. Judge Kelly stated that while police and investigators can sometimes circumvent the law in order to prevent the commission of a crime (*ugh!*), thereby avoiding a greater evil, that justification cannot be applied to government prosecutors whose actions are "entirely unrelated to detecting crime."

Judge Kelly's groundbreaking ruling outraged the government.

The entire Tenth Circuit reheard the case and vacated the three-judge panel's unanimous decision, thereby returning America to a system where the government can place itself above the law. The court's reliance on the fact that plea-bargaining is a "historic practice" is a ridiculous contention, given that vote buying, bribery of public officials, and other forms of public corruption have also been historic practices since ancient times.

The court also subscribed to several other nonsensical government arguments. The court had difficulty reading a seven-letter word: "whoever." First, it somehow managed to conclude that the meaning of "whoever"—"whatever person; any person" according to Webster's—was not "clear and indisputable." Next, it managed to invent the idea that a statute only applies to the government when the government is specifically mentioned in the statute. The court accordingly "reasoned" that "whoever" doesn't really mean "whoever," and claimed that this was "clear, unmistakable, and unarguable language!"

HOW TO BUY A MURDERER

The federal government claims the power to decide whether some criminals are more morally repugnant than others. When the government breaks the law in order to bribe a mass murderer for his testimony against another individual who it thinks is more dangerous to society, the entire criminal justice system loses credibility. Not only should the government prosecute the bribed witness to the full extent of the law, but also the government should prosecute *its own attorneys* for violating the criminal bribery law. Failing that demonstrates the government is not interested in justice, just victory; not fairness, just force.

A recipient of extraordinary government bribery once told a jury: "I never killed in a fit of anger. I'm controlled. A professional. I killed because of my oath." Those words were spoken by Salvatore "Sammy the Bull" Gravano, the underboss in the Gambino crime family, who confessed to nineteen cold-blooded murders.

Rather than prosecuting Gravano so that he didn't have a chance to commit his twentieth murder, the government bribed him for his testimony against individuals who it felt were even more heinous criminals. Because the government made an illegal deal—clearly in violation of the statute criminalizing the buying of witness testimony—with Gravano, the government allowed Gravano to be imprisoned for a mere *five-year* sentence for his nineteen murders.

At twenty-three, Gravano joined a crime family and began running a loan sharking operation. Shortly thereafter, he was given orders to commit his first murder. He describes it in his autobiography: "I smelt the gunpowder. The noise was deafening. Now I saw his head jerk back, his body convulse and slip sideways. I saw the blood. . . . He looked like he was sleeping. He looked peaceful. You going to blow me away now?

I thought." After proving his worth, Gravano joined the Gambino crime family and became "made" in 1976. Over a fourteen-year period, he admitted to a total of eight murders.

As Paul Castellano became the boss, there was significant division within the leadership of the Gambino family.

John Gotti, one of the top-ranking members of the family, was angered that he had been passed up and vowed to eliminate Castellano. During this time, Gotti realized that Gravano was an asset and made him a member of his inner circle. The two spent ten months planning a hit on Castellano, which culminated when their eight hit men gunned down Castellano in front of Sparks Steakhouse in midtown Manhattan on December 16, 1985. Gotti and Gravano watched the murder sitting a block away in a black car with tinted windows, and then cruised the scene joyfully to observe the maimed corpses.

With Castellano gone, Gotti took over the leadership of the Gambino crime family and installed Gravano as the *consigliere*, the family's number-three position. In a six-year period of working under Gotti, Gravano claims he carried out eleven murders, in addition to the eight he had already performed. Gravano eventually became Gotti's underboss—the number-two slot—and heir to the leadership.

The federal government had thrice failed to convict Gotti for committing violent crimes. Law enforcement had been wiretapping the conversations of Gotti and Gravano for years and had gained valuable information because Gotti had a tendency to boast about his crimes—including the Castellano murder—rather than keeping quiet about them. Their downfall began when they were arrested together on December 11, 1990.

Gravano became angered that Gotti's own mouth had precipitated their arrests and sensed that Gotti would proclaim his innocence and allow Gravano to take the fall for all of their crimes. Gravano's fears were confirmed when Gotti handpicked their defense team and refused to allow Gravano to sever his case and have his own lawyers. So, on

October 10, 1991, Gravano sent word to the FBI that he was ready to talk.

The government, in complete violation of the witness bribery statute, made Gravano an offer that he couldn't refuse. The government purchased Gravano's testimony against Gotti and high-ranking members of several other New York City crime families. In exchange, Gravano's freedom was granted: his reward was a mere five-years imprisonment—barely more than three months per murder.

Beginning on March 2, 1992, the Gotti jury heard nine full days of testimony from Gravano about Gotti's culpability for the Castellano murder. The government's case hinged primarily on the testimony of this bribed witness, and accordingly, Gotti was convicted and sentenced to multiple life terms without any possibility of parole. He died in prison.

At Gravano's sentencing, Gotti's chief prosecutor, by then, and now, himself a federal judge, told the court that Gravano had "rendered extraordinary, unprecedented, historic assistance to the government." As noble as fighting organized crime may be, the government is not above the law and cannot legally purchase testimony from witnesses. It is debatable how noble its goals even were, since it spared one man who committed nineteen murders to convict another man of one murder, the victim of which was himself a murdering mob boss. It is patently obvious that Gravano had a motivation to lie, exaggerate, and fabricate Gotti's responsibility in the Castellano murder while downplaying his own role. Justice is simply not served when a government witness is encouraged to say under oath only what the government wants to hear and then gets his life spared by blaming his crimes on somebody else.

BOMBERS GET THE BIG BUCKS

When the federal government isn't luring a murderer of nineteen to testify by offering a mere five years in jail, it may be making terrorists into instant millionaires. Emad Salem served as a technical officer in the Egyptian Army for seventeen years before immigrating to the United States in 1987. He had difficulty coming to terms with his new existence as a taxi driver and a stock boy and proceeded to develop fabricated stories about his previous life.

Among the lies, Salem morphed himself into an Egyptian military intelligence officer who served as a double agent and one of President Anwar Sadat's bodyguards. He also told the FBI that he knew Muammar el-Qaddafi of Libya, Saddam Hussein of Iraq, and King Hussein of Jordan. He even lied under oath, testimony he later admitted was perjured, at a criminal trial claiming that he was wounded in 1981 trying to protect President Sadat when he was assassinated! Salem later testified in court that the lying campaign actually began when he met a woman whom he later married: "I was trying to impress her. I told her a lot of bragging stories."

The FBI became aware of Salem's lies and tried to recruit him to infiltrate the circle around an Egyptian terrorist who had gunned down Rabbi Meir Kahane, the founder of the Jewish Defense League. In October 1991, Salem agreed to serve as an FBI informant and was paid a salary of five hundred dollars per week.

Salem infiltrated the circle of Sheik Omar Abdel Rahman (the "blind sheik") and ten other Islamic men as they were plotting to bomb the World Trade Center, the United Nations, the FBI offices in New York City, and the Lincoln and Holland Tunnels. At some point, Salem became a rogue informant and began acting as an *agent provocateur.*

Salem's tape recordings demonstrate that he drafted bombing plans for Sheik Abdel Rahman for the February 1993 World Trade Center bombing, most likely out of sheer greed. In the summer of 1992, Salem told the FBI of the bombing plot, but the FBI didn't believe Salem because he had recently failed a series of lie-detector tests. Not trusting his credibility and not wanting to pay the exorbitant fees he demanded, the FBI dropped Salem as an informant.

The bombing was carried out on February 26, 1993. Two days after the bombing, the FBI approached Salem for his help in solving the case. The FBI should have been very skeptical of Salem, who did nothing to prevent the bombing. One possible motive for Salem's failure to stop the bombing is greed: He had information that the FBI refused to buy and wanted to save it until the price was right. Another possible motive is terrorism: Salem actually organized the plot and built the bomb but walked away clean by implicating his accomplices.

Regardless of the scenario, Salem's credibility as a witness against Shiek Abdel Rahman and the other ten men was shattered. Yet, the FBI once again violated the law prohibiting the purchase of witness testimony and agreed to pay Salem *over one million dollars* ($1,056,200 to be exact) for his testimony! Salem could have been Congress' poster boy when it wrote the anti-bribery law, since it is hard to imagine a less credible witness than a known perjurer who successfully extorted money out of the FBI. It is amazing that such an individual remained on the federal government's payroll rather than in its penitentiaries.

THE PIMP STAYS IN THE PICTURE

The federal government illegally bribed a brothel baron to help it bring down a bigger target. Joseph Conforte owned an infamous Reno, Nevada, brothel called the Mustang Ranch. His past is filled with brushes with the law, beginning with an extortion conviction in 1959. Those charges stemmed out of his threat go public with news that the district attorney had sexual relations with a minor. A 1976 grand jury report detailed how Conforte bribed local officials with free brothel passes and campaign contributions.

After failing to pay withholding taxes, Conforte was convicted of tax evasion in 1977 and was sentenced to a prison term of twenty years. When his appeal was denied in 1980, he forfeited his forty-thousand-dollar bail and fled to Rio de Janeiro, Brazil, where be purchased a penthouse apartment overlooking the beach.

Around that time, U.S. District Judge Harry Claiborne, a federal judge in Nevada, had been outspokenly critical of federal prosecutors who were overzealously trying to crack down on Nevada's vices. Unlikely to be a mere coincidence, federal prosecutors soon began an investigation of a judge who had issued rulings unfavorable to the government. Amidst their investigation, the federal prosecutors received a telephone call from Brazil. It was Conforte, claiming that he paid a total of eighty-five thousand dollars in bribes to Judge Claiborne in exchange for favorable rulings in pending cases.

The prosecutors proceeded to negotiate a deal with Conforte in order to secure his testimony against Judge Claiborne. The government compensated Conforte by reducing his twenty-year prison term to fifteen months and dropping the pending federal bail-jumping charges against him. In April 1984, the government put the convicted felon and brothel owner on the stand to testify against Judge Claiborne. Upon cross-examination, Judge Claiborne's defense attorney demonstrated that Confonte was in New York at the time when he supposedly was paying the bribes in Nevada.

The jury failed to convict Judge Claiborne (the jurors reported that all but two believed him to be actually innocent), and the government decided to drop the bribery charges. The federal government subsequently tried the judge for evading approximately a hundred thousand dollars in income tax payments, totally unrelated to his alleged receipt of the bribes. Judge Claiborne was eventually impeached and removed from office, after refusing to resign while he served eighteen months in prison.

In Judge Claiborne's first trial, a jury failed to believe the testimony of the bribed government witness. However, justice was not served. The federal prosecutors, in paying for Conforte's testimony, committed the same crime—bribery—as they charged the defendant had committed!

Of course, the prosecutors were never tried for witness bribery. And why didn't the federal government ever investigate their motives? Nothing good was accomplished by reducing a brothel owner's sentence by eighteen years in order to prosecute *unsuccessfully* a politically unpopular federal judge. But the prosecutors got to show their power: the power to indict, the power to prosecute, and the power to break the laws they'd sworn to uphold.

INCENTIVE TO LIE

The victims of government bribery range from a federal judge to a basketball superstar. On July 18, 2003, prosecutors accused Los Angeles Laker Kobe Bryant of sexually assaulting a nineteen-year-old woman in Eagle, Colorado. Bryant maintained his innocence and claimed that he had consensual sex with the accuser.

The State of Colorado has compensated the accuser to the point where she has a pecuniary interest in the government's conviction of Bryant. A transcript of a June 21, 2004, hearing reveals allegations that the accuser received almost $20,000 from the Colorado Crime Victim's Compensation program. The state paid $17,000 in mental health expenses and $2,300 in lost wages to the accuser, despite the fact that rape victims are generally limited to $1,125 for mental health reimbursement.

Because a crime victim who makes a material misrepresentation is disqualified from receiving victim's compensation, the accuser signed a contract agreeing to pay back the money "if falsehoods were discovered." "Falsehoods" here would mean "testimony harmful to the government."

The accuser has already made statements accusing Bryant of sexually assaulting her. If these statements are false, she has an enormous "motivation to persist in the false allegation," defense attorney Pamela Mackey told the court. Thus, if a jury finds that the sexual assault never happened, the accuser stands to lose twenty grand. How can the government seek not only to put this woman on the witness stand knowing she has a motivation to commit perjury, but also try to prevent the jury from hearing that the government has paid a substantial sum of money to her?

We will never know. On September 1, 2004, the government asked the court to dismiss its own case against Bryant; and the court did so.

GOVERNMENT AS LAWBREAKER

Supreme Court Justice Louis Brandeis wrote in his 1928 *Olmstead v. United States* dissent, "Decency, security, and liberty alike demand that government officials shall be subjected to the same rules of conduct that are commands to the citizen. In a government of laws, existence of the government will be imperiled if it fails to observe the law scrupulously. Our government is the potent, the omnipresent teacher. For good or for ill, it teaches the whole people by its example. Crime is contagious. If the government becomes a lawbreaker, it breeds contempt for law; it invites every man to become a law unto himself; it invites anarchy. To declare that in the administration of the criminal law the end justifies the means—to declare that the government may commit crimes in order to secure the conviction of a private criminal—would bring terrible retribution."

8

ASSAULTING
THE PEOPLE

She ordered her agents to inject poisonous gas into a building, after using armored tanks to raid and destroy the building. When the building caught on fire, her agents shot and killed people who tried to save their own lives by fleeing the flames. She refused to allow the fire department to rescue those trapped inside. In the end, eighty-six innocent men, women, children, and babies died from the cyanide poisoning, the bullets, and the tanks. Most were reduced to ash.

Given the female pronoun, readers should be able to guess that the person responsible for this massacre was not Osama bin Laden or Timothy McVeigh. No, the perpetrator was the chief law enforcement officer of the United States, Attorney General Janet Reno (other outrages by whom we covered in Chapter Two).

The attorney general used the U.S. military to engage in warfare, to murder scores of innocent American civilians, and then she orchestrated an elaborate cover-up so that the American people could never hear the truth. Janet Reno—with the blood of eighty-six innocent people on her hands—should not only have been fired from her job, but also should have been indicted for nearly ninety counts of murder. Yet, because Janet Reno was "the government," she managed to walk away blameless from this massacre.

MURDER IN WACO

David Koresh and his followers lived in a small religious community at Mount Carmel, a ranch complex in a rural area near Waco, Texas. Decades ago, this apocalyptic group, called the Branch Davidians, split from the Seventh Day Adventist Church and established their settlement in Waco. Men, women, and children lived in a large communal house that was situated on seventy-seven acres of flat prairie land.

In early 1993, the newly inaugurated Clinton administration was facing the possibility that Congress might scale back the Bureau of Alcohol, Tobacco and Firearms (BATF), a law enforcement agency devoted to enforcing, among other things, federal gun laws. The Clinton administration, opposing any effort to reduce the size of the government, decided to portray the Branch Davidians as a cult and have the BATF declare war on the group. The government hyped up media interviews with former and disgruntled members of the group—not exactly the most credible sources—who accused the Davidians of being polygamists and child abusers. But this wasn't enough.

The Clinton administration concocted an illegal weapons case in order to convince a federal judge to sign off on a warrant to search the Mount Carmel complex. The government's case at best was that the Davidians had failed to comply with *taxes* on machine guns! The government alleged that a package of grenade casings had been shipped to the complex, and that the Davidians were converting semi-automatic weapons into automatic weapons without a license. Both of these allegations were later determined to be patently false. The grenade casing shipment turned out to be fake, collectible items. And the Davidians had a lawful contract with a licensed gun dealer to assemble automatic rifles from semi-automatic rifles.

In order to enforce this machine gun tax, the government considered two methods for serving the search warrant: raid and siege.

The government claimed that a "dynamic raid" was necessary to prevent the Davidians from destroying evidence of the automatic rifle conversions. The BATF had received training from the U.S. Army Special Forces and practiced large-scale raids in preparation for a February 28, 1993, raid of Mount Carmel.

"Operation Trojan Horse" (how the government loves these names!) began that morning, with federal agents, and fifteen members of the U.S. military, approaching the complex while disguised as ranchers hauling cattle trailers. Three unmarked black U.S. Army helicopters hovered over the complex and even fired shots at the compound. When David Koresh answered the door to investigate the situation, the federal agents opened fire on the building and the Davidians defended themselves. Except for their gunshots causing the deaths of five Davidians, including one child, the government retreated because its raid was proving "unsuccessful."

Four BATF agents, who entered into the building through the roof to throw grenades blindly into the complex, died as a result of the Davidians trying to defend themselves. In 1994, four Davidians were tried for conspiracy to murder these agents and were acquitted by a jury.

Reacting to the deaths of the four federal agents, President Clinton declared war on the Davidians by ordering a "quazi-military" siege. During a standoff that lasted fifty-one days, the FBI, the Texas National Guard, and the Army Reserves encircled the building.

After negotiations, Koresh agreed to surrender, but the FBI bailed out of the agreement and refused to comply with its end of the bargain. The FBI proceeded to engage in a psychological warfare campaign, illegally shutting off the building's electricity and blockading all means of electronic communication. Agents installed loudspeakers to broadcast, all day and night, high decibel noises of birds squawking, sirens, rabbits being slaughtered, rock music, and Tibetan monk chants.

Then, tired of eating pizza for seven weeks in front of Mount Carmel, the government was ready to wipe out the Davidians once and for all. An FBI spokesman declared, "We are going to show them that we control the compound and they are impotent." Is the government interested in achieving justice or showing its power?

On April 19, 1993, Janet Reno approved a 568-page final assault plan to be used against the Davidians. Armored Bradley Fighting Vehicles busted the exterior walls of the building so that the FBI could inject flammable gas grenades throughout the building. The federal agents fired bullets upon the individuals who tried to flee the complex! Wasn't the whole purpose of the FBI presence to get the Davidians to come out?

Shortly thereafter, the entire building was enveloped by an enormous fireball. It is unclear how the fire began, but a commonly accepted proposition is that a lantern was ignited due to the government unsafely injecting the flammable gas into the building on a day when the wind speed exceeded thirty miles per hour. Some evidence also suggests that U.S. Military Special Operations detonated fifty-five gallons of petroleum jet fuel inside the compound. The FBI refused to allow the local fire departments near the complex, thereby eliminating any chance that those eighty-six innocent men, women, children, and babies could have survived.

The use of the Bradley tanks marked the first time since the Civil War that the federal government used tanks on Americans.

Janet Reno's investigation developed a preposterous claim that Koresh set the building ablaze as a suicidal act to prevent the government from capturing him. While not in magnitude, certainly in substance, this theory ranks alongside the denials of the Holocaust. Autopsy photographs reveal that many of the deaths were uniquely attributed to cyanide poisoning, which results when CS gas, which the U.S. military injected into the compound, is burned. Additionally, the women and children who were hiding in an underground crawlspace had their skulls crushed when the Bradley tanks emerged into the building. It is likely that many of the eighty-six individuals had died before the building went ablaze, and that the fire merely allowed the government to conceal much of the evidence implicating itself in the massacre.

Reno, the child-abuse advocate from Miami, Florida, trumped up the need for an imminent assault on Mount Carmel by alleging that Koresh was sexually molesting children inside the complex. *Reno herself eventually determined these allegations were false,* yet went ahead with the plan. In so doing, she allowed twenty-four innocent children and babies to die of cyanide poisoning and skull fractures from military tanks.

For six years, the Reno Justice Department covered up the fact that incendiary poisonous gas rounds were fired into the building. Because such evidence would destroy the credibility of the government's assertion that Koresh intentionally set the building ablaze, it is no surprise that Reno would want to hide evidence that would implicate her in the murder of eighty-six innocent civilians.

Representative Dan Burton, chairman of the House Committee on Government Reform, stated that Janet Reno was directly responsible for concealing this evidence. Burton further explained how Reno directed Texas law enforcement agencies and the Texas National Guard to remain mum and keep the truth "under lock and key." While Reno disclosed information about the FBI's use of "pyrotechnic devices" against the Davidians, she miraculously continues to deny that the government was involved in the fire.

Despite her blatant lies, cover-ups, and misrepresentations, Janet Reno was never investigated. She politically weaseled her way out of the situation in 1999 by appointing a special prosecutor, yet limiting the scope of his investigation. Additionally, she told the prosecutor that his second-in-command would be Reno-ally Edward Dowd, who on *the previous day* Reno had cleared of a criminal probe stemming from charges for using federal money for a political campaign. How impartial do you think he was?

The investigators ducked all of the questions about Reno and the FBI's blunders. However, they managed to find a "good guy" to serve as the government's scapegoat: an assistant U.S. Attorney who blew the whistle on the FBI's destruction of evidence when attempting to prosecute some of the surviving Davidians.

There was never any investigation of Janet Reno's use of the U.S. military against American civilians. Her doing so is a clear violation of the Posse Comitatus Act, which prohibits the president and his subordinates from authorizing the military to engage in civilian law enforcement unless authorized by Congress. The American people deserve an explanation of why Janet Reno authorized the use of Delta Forces, Special Operations, National Guard, and Army helicopters in order to enforce a citizen's obligation to pay taxes on a machine gun!

Rather than being investigated, charged, and fired, federal agents involved in the massacre were rewarded with promotions. Why was there never any federal investigation as to the involvement of Janet Reno, and even Bill Clinton, in the massacre?

We'll never ultimately know whether Janet Reno is guilty of murdering those eighty-six innocent civilians, but there is certainly sufficient evidence to warrant an indictment against her and to have a jury hear the evidence against her. The day after the massacre, President Clinton verbosely announced, "I was, frankly, surprised would be a mild word, to say that anyone that would suggest that the attorney general should resign because some religious fanatics murdered themselves."

KIDNAPPED IN MIAMI

Seven years later, Janet Reno flipped over to a different page of the penal code. Rather than condemning the murder of twenty-four children, this children's rights advocate illegally kidnapped a six-year-old boy at gunpoint.

In November 1999, Elizabet Gonzalez and her six-year-old son Elian decided to flee Fidel Castro's tyrannical and oppressive regime in Cuba so they could begin a new life in America. During the journey, their motorboat encountered rough seas and capsized. Treading in the shark-infested water, Elizabet, in order to save Elian, bounded him to an inner-tube and prayed, "The only thing I am asking you is to make sure Elian reaches

American soil—that Elian reaches a land of liberty." Right before his eyes, Elian witnessed his mother, along with ten others on the boat, drown in the sea. Elian drifted in the inner tube for two days, before he was spotted off the coast of Fort Lauderdale and brought ashore on Thanksgiving Day by a fisherman.

Elian's relatives, great uncle Lazaro Gonzales and several cousins, who had previously fled Castro's regime, embraced the boy and were overjoyed to raise him in Miami.

Back in Cuba, Juan Miguel Gonzalez, Elian's biological father and an active member of Castro's Communist Party, couldn't bear to see his son grow up in a free country. Castro mobilized anti-American sentiments by holding rallies in Havana on behalf of Juan Miguel and put pressure on the Clinton administration to return Elian to Castro's tyranny.

Seemingly sympathetic to a dictatorial Communist regime, Bill Clinton and Janet Reno selected the worst possible ending to Elian's miraculous survival story. In January 2000, the Reno Justice Department ordered the Immigration and Naturalization Service (INS) to send Elian back into the hands of Fidel Castro.

Elian Gonzalez's case was nothing more than a custody dispute and should have been handled as such. In Florida, as in all states, custody disputes are addressed by state family courts, do not involve the Justice Department, and focus on one paramount issue: What are the best interests of the child—not the interests of a parent, not the interests of a president, not the interests of a foreign government. The INS refused to consider what would be in the best interests of *Elian* and was primarily concerned with the default rights of *Elian's father* to raise his biological child.

Never before has there ever been a case of a child's custody being changed by the force of the federal government without a specific court order authorizing it. On January 10, 2000, Lazaro Gonzalez applied for asylum in the United States on behalf of Elian and requested that the INS be enjoined from deporting Elian until the asylum matter was resolved. A federal district judge denied Elian's asylum application on the basis of an INS determination, without making any independent findings and refusing to second-guess the motives of the Clinton administration, that a six-year-old was too young to be granted asylum against his father's wishes.

Lazaro Gonzalez appealed this decision to the U.S. Court of Appeals for the Eleventh Circuit. On April 6, Fidel Castro sent Elian's father to Washington, D.C., since the INS wanted Elian to stay in Juan Miguel's custody while Elian remained in the United States. Recognizing that Lazaro rather than Juan Miguel was Elian's proper adult representative, on April 19, the Court of Appeals for the Eleventh Circuit enjoined the government from moving Elian Gonzalez outside the jurisdiction of U.S. courts, specifically, to the Cuban diplomatic mission in Washington, until the court issued its ruling on the merits of Elian's case.

Janet Reno simply couldn't accept the fact that Elian could live in a free nation with caring Uncle Lazaro until his appeal was ruled upon.

In direct violation of the Eleventh Circuit's order, on April 22, Reno ordered the INS illegally to kidnap Elian at gunpoint. In a pre-dawn raid of Lazaro Gonzalez's house, a SWAT team of twenty-five INS agents busted down the front door, fired pepper spray into the surrounding crowd, and ransacked the house. After opening a closet to find the fisherman who had saved Elian holding the crying child in his arms, a federal agent aimed his assault weapon at Elian and ordered the fisherman to "Give me the boy or I'll shoot you!" The agents quickly carried the screaming Elian out of the home and drove him away in an unmarked car.

In its typical secretive fashion, the Clinton administration sought to cover up this outrageous kidnapping. The first agent to enter the Gonzalez home kicked, maced, and assaulted an NBC cameraman, ensuring there was no video footage of the agents ransacking the house and seizing Elian. But Associated Press photographer Albert Diaz was hiding in a bedroom. He positioned himself in time to take the shot seen round the world: a federal agent aiming an automatic weapon at the chest of a six-year-old boy.

Rather than condemning the illegal actions of his corrupt attorney general, Bill Clinton praised Janet Reno: "The law was upheld and that was the right thing to do." While the INS agents had a search warrant to enter Lazaro Gonzalez's home, a detailed review of that warrant revealed the entire seizure to be a charade.

"It was not a warrant to seize the child. Elian was not lost, and it is a semantic sleight of hand to compare his forcible removal to the seizure of evidence, which is what a search warrant is for," Harvard Law School Professor Laurence Tribe declared.

Janet Reno and the federal government had absolutely no judicial authority for entering into a private home to seize a child. Just as a father who was awarded custody of his child could not break into the home of the child's mother to seize the child, the INS had no right to enter the home of Lazaro Gonzalez. Put simply, Janet Reno decided to take the law, and Elian, into her own hands.

It is clear that the "search" warrant was just a pretext to get into Lazaro Gonzalez's house. No legitimate federal purpose was served by the raid. Elian was lovingly cared for by blood relatives; he was not "involuntarily restrained"; and a federal appeals court was soon to hear his appeal of the federal trial judge's denial of his right to apply for asylum. A simple court order, sought with notice to Elian's lawyers, could have peacefully transferred custody.

And Reno's scandalous actions don't end with violating the *terms* of the search warrant. The warrant *itself* demonstrated that the Clinton administration, no surprise, lied to the American people. A review of the affidavit on which the warrant was based shows that the raid was constitutionally flawed, unlawful, and repugnant to the language and spirit of the then three-day-old decision of the Eleventh Circuit that *ordered* Ms. Reno to keep Elian in the U.S. and *denied* her request for an injunction requiring Mr. Gonzalez to turn the boy over.

In order to conceal the truth and obtain an illegal search warrant, Reno had the INS capitalize on a judicial loophole. The Immigration and Naturalization Service didn't seek the warrant from Judge Michael Moore, the federal district judge in Miami handling the case. Rather, the INS waited until after 7:00 P.M. on Good Friday, when a federal duty magistrate, not familiar with the case and notoriously pro-government in his rulings, was available to hear warrant applications.

The affidavit presented to the magistrate was signed by Special Agent Mary Rodriguez of the INS. Ms. Rodriguez told the magistrate that Elian was being "concealed" at Lazaro's home, that the boy was "unlawfully restrained" there, and that INS Deputy Director of Investigations James T. Spearman Jr. had already ordered the arrest of Elian because the boy was "an illegal alien." In response, the magistrate issued a search warrant.

Thus the power that the government invoked to invade the house was that conferred by Congress when contraband or evidence of a crime is being hidden. That was hardly the case with Elian, who was often present, for all the world to see, in Lazaro Gonzalez's front yard. Moreover, *the INS itself* had designated Lazaro Gonzalez as Elian's guardian and had placed the boy in his great-uncle's house.

What the affidavit omits is as revealing as what it says. Janet Reno justified her agents' use of tear gas, guns, and violence by claiming a fear of weapons in Lazaro's house. Agent Rodriguez's affidavit says nothing of the kind. Reno claims she seized the child for his own best interests. There is no allegation in Rodriguez's affidavit of mistreatment or likely harm to Elian by his Miami relatives. Rodriguez also didn't tell the magistrate that Aaron Podhurst, a well-respected Miami lawyer and a longtime friend of Reno, was feverishly mediating negotiations between lawyers for the government, Elian's father, and Lazaro Gonzalez, even as the affidavit was being filed.

The application for the warrant was also troubling because the INS never arrests Cuban aliens without evidence that they have committed a crime. This restraint on the part of the INS is consistent with the Cuban

Adjustment Act of 1966, which makes Cuban nationals eligible for U.S. citizenship once they've been in the U.S. for a year. Yet, Janet Reno and Bill Clinton decided to make a little six-year-old boy a political pawn so that they could appease a Communist dictator.

Janet Reno should have been indicted for forcefully and illegally kidnapping a six-year-old at gunpoint. The raid on Lazaro Gonzalez's home was nothing short of a criminal act of brute violence. Our nation is no more free than Fidel Castro's Cuba when our leaders resort to Gestapo-like tactics in order to enforce what they say is "the law."

On June 28, 2000, the INS cleared the way for Elian's return to Cuba after the Supreme Court declined to get involved in the case. Janet Reno praised the Court's decision (or lack thereof): "I hope that everyone will . . . join me in wishing this family, and this special little boy, well." Janet Reno probably jumped for joy, knowing that Elian would be raised under another government whose top officials disregard the rule of law and even murder and kidnap innocent children.

TRAPPING, KILLING, JUSTIFYING

As bad as Reno is, she is not alone in trampling the law, and Waco was not the only example of the federal government declaring war on a group of different people minding their own business.

Randy Weaver lived with his wife, children, and a family friend, Kevin Harris, on a twenty-acre parcel of property in rural Idaho called Ruby Ridge. The government, with no better use for taxpayer money and with no regard for the Bill of Rights, decided to investigate Weaver for *being* a white separatist. In 1989, the FBI and the BATF set up a sting operation in order to blackmail and entrap Weaver into buying sawed-off shotguns. Weaver repeatedly refused, but eventually broke down and purchased two shotguns. He was indicted on a weapons charge and missed his February 1991 court appearance.

Because Weaver refused to appear in court for this weapons violation, the government conducted an elaborate eighteen-month military siege of Weaver's land on Ruby Ridge. According to a *Wall Street Journal* report, "The U.S. marshals called in military aerial reconnaissance and had photos studied by the Defense Mapping Agency. . . . They had psychological profiles performed and installed $130,000 worth of solar-powered long-range spy cameras. They intercepted the Weavers' mail. They even knew the menstrual cycle of Weaver's teenage daughter, and planned an arrest scenario around it."

In final preparation for the siege, the federal government brought in four hundred law enforcement agents who were armed with automatic weapons, sniper rifles, and night vision scopes. All of this was necessary to defend themselves against two men—with no history of violence—armed only with shotguns? On August 21, 1992, six members of a paramilitary unit of the U.S. Marshals Service went onto Weaver's property to conduct undercover surveillance; the family dog started to bark wildly upon noticing the marshals.

A marshal proceeded to shoot the dog, causing Kevin Harris and Weaver's fourteen-year-old son, Sammy, to grab their shotguns in self-defense. A firefight broke out, and a marshal fired a fatal shot at Sammy *in the back* as he was trying to run back into the cabin. Harris, firing at the marshals in self-defense, ended up killing one of them. Years later, a federal jury would *acquit* Harris on murder charges because the jury found that he had properly invoked his right to self-defense.

The marshals retreated and called in FBI snipers to take positions and surround the Weaver cabin. Larry Potts, the FBI supervisor at the Washington, D.C., headquarters, then instituted a dramatic and illegal change to the FBI's rules of engagement. FBI guidelines permit agents to use deadly force only when necessary to defend themselves against *imminent* attacks. With utter disregard for the law, Potts issued a "shoot to kill" order instructing agents that they "could and should" shoot *any armed adult male*. Potts justified this usurpation of the law by stating that Weaver and Harris often carried guns on their own property; such gun possession is completely legal under Idaho law. Additionally, the FBI had never announced its presence and had never offered the men an opportunity to surrender peacefully.

The following morning, Weaver left the cabin to visit his son's body. He was shot and wounded *from behind* by FBI sniper Lon Horiuchi. As Weaver was struggling back into the cabin, his wife Vicki stood in the doorway holding their ten-month-old baby in her arms. Moments later, Horiuchi fired a fatal shot into *Vicki's head*, as she held the baby. The FBI tried to claim that the murder was an accident, but Horiuchi later testified in court that he was an accurate shot at two hundred yards.

The day after Vicki's murder, the FBI agents taunted the family, saying, "Good morning, Mrs. Weaver. We had pancakes for breakfast. What did you have?" And after an eleven-day standoff, Weaver and Harris finally surrendered.

The federal government proceeded to charge Weaver and Harris with conspiring to murder the U.S. marshal. The Department of Justice asked for the death penalty. The government employed the media to engage in a propaganda war; the *New York Times* described Weaver and his family as "an armed separatist brigade."

It didn't play.

In July 1993, a jury accepted their pleas of self-defense and found them innocent on each of the serious criminal charges. But there was still good news for the government: Weaver was convicted on the original weapons charge! These rogue FBI agents must have been proud of their work killing a man's wife and son while trying to kill him twice, just to bring him to "justice" for buying two sawed-off shotguns that they sold to him. The government eventually paid the Weaver family $3.1 million to settle a wrongful death action.

As a result of pressure from President Bill Clinton and FBI Director Louis Freeh, FBI sniper Lon Horiuchi got away with murder. Horiuchi, who illegally shot Weaver and then proceeded to murder Weaver's wife, never even had to stand trial. A local Idaho prosecutor brought an involuntary manslaughter charge against Horiuchi, which prompted outrage among high-ranking Clinton administration officials who wanted to discipline, or not discipline, their own agents.

In order to prevent Horiuchi's prosecution, the federal government sued the Idaho prosecutor.

Bill Clinton dispatched his solicitor general, Seth Waxman, to the U.S. Court of Appeals for the Ninth Circuit to make the argument that the Constitution prevents a state from prosecuting a federal agent for lawfully carrying out his official duties. Bill Clinton's fascination with the case is suspicious; as well, it is unprecedented for the solicitor general personally to argue a lower court case.

The court rejected the government's fallacious argument that Horiuchi was somehow immune from murdering Vicki Weaver because he claimed that he was just following orders. Judge Alex Kozinski wrote for the court, "Immunity has limits. When an agent acts in an objectively unreasonable manner, those limits are exceeded, and a state may bring a criminal prosecution."

Apparently Horiuchi didn't learn his lesson from the Nuremberg and Lieutenant Calley prosecutions that the claim "I was just following orders" is a patently unacceptable excuse for killing innocent people. Not only did Horiuchi unlawfully seize on his "license to kill," but he even violated the FBI's *illegal* rules of engagement! Even the illegal FBI rules prohibited agents from shooting when it would endanger children, and commanded the killing of armed adult males, yet Horiuchi fired a bullet into the head of an unarmed woman holding her baby.

In spite of the Idaho prosecutor's power to prosecute, Horiuchi became a free man before his trial happened. A new county prosecutor was elected, and the Clinton administration persuaded the new prosecutor to drop the case because it was time to "move on."

FBI Director Louis Freeh refused to investigate the case seriously, and instead engaged in a massive cover-up. It is preposterous that the federal government did not prosecute a single agent, from Horiuchi and the U.S.

marshal who killed Weaver's son to the FBI field commanders who authorized their snipers illegally to fire their weapons. Yet the federal government tried to convict Weaver and Harris of capital murder.

Larry Potts, who was in charge of the operation, received a promotion rather than a prosecution! Even after the Justice Department released a report stating that Potts overstepped the Constitution in "encourag[ing] the use of deadly force," Freeh named Potts to the number-two post in the FBI, deputy director; the Senate Judiciary Committee sharply criticized Freeh for exhibiting such "questionable judgment."

Apparently, being a federal official means you have a license to kill—or at least immunity from prosecution for murder.

PART 2
WAKE-UP CALL

9

PERSONAL ODYSSEY

Let's take a break from this parade of horrors and get a little personal. Winston Churchill once famously said, "Any man under thirty who is not a liberal has no heart, and any man over thirty who is not a conservative has no brains."

In my case, things didn't work quite that way.

As an undergraduate at Princeton in the late sixties and early seventies, and later as a law student at Notre Dame, I was a strong and vocal conservative. At the height of the anti-Vietnam War movement, I arranged a campus visit to Princeton by William F. Buckley Jr., the leading conservative intellectual at the time. I brought in other speakers, moderated panels, orchestrated rallies, and made no secret of my political views. I even once wore a T-shirt in 1970 that proclaimed "Bomb Hanoi"! I thought Richard Nixon's law-and-order, pro-police platforms in 1968 and 1972 were right for the country.

Fast-forward two decades, however, and you will find me as a judge invalidating police drunk-driving roadblocks in New Jersey and forbidding the cops from stopping someone on a whim. Before my ruling, the police could stop and search any cars they wished. They didn't need any rationale—you didn't even have to be driving erratically—they just stopped cars because they had the power to do so. My published opinion, which ruled that such stops were illegal in the absence of some demonstration of illegal behavior—like weaving in and out of traffic or bolting out of a bar's parking lot—was upheld by the appellate courts, and today in New Jersey random stops by police are illegal, and any evidence acquired during them is supposed to be excluded from trial.

I am proud of that opinion. But it is one that I would have railed against as a conservative college student and law student and as an active Republican practicing attorney. My younger self would have said, "So what's the problem? If you're not driving under the influence, what does it matter if the police stop and search you? Think of all the drunk drivers those stops will get off the road."

It is not an unreasonable argument: Why not give up a little personal liberty—like the right to drive your car without being stopped by the police on a whim—in return for temporary safety—like fewer drunks on the road? If the random stops keep one drunk driver off the road and save one child's life, isn't it worth the inconvenience?

Don't be like the younger me. Don't be too quick to answer. Consider first Benjamin Franklin's famous pronouncement: "They that can give up essential liberty to obtain a little temporary safety deserve neither liberty nor safety."

Ouch!

Is driving a car without being pulled over by the police an "essential liberty"? Will the drunk drivers that such pulls-over find give you a "little temporary safety"? These are not trivial questions. When Franklin made his pronouncement in 1759, he certainly didn't think similar questions of the day were trivial. And that was back when there was no country, no Constitution, and no guarantees of liberty.

The Constitution says the government cannot *arrest you* without probable cause—specific evidence that you more likely than not committed a specific crime. And our courts have uniformly held that police can't *stop you* without articulable suspicion—reasons that can be stated as to why your behavior is suspicious of criminal activity. Think about it: If the police can stop you for *any reason*, then they can stop you for *the wrong reason*, like race or appearance or religion or politics or personal vendetta, just as the SS and the KGB did to persons in Nazi Germany and in the Soviet Union.

So why my change in philosophy and outlook? What caused me to flip from being a law-and-order conservative to a rugged individualist? The answer: My eight years on the bench.

GROWING PAINS

It took a while, but over time I learned that once the police have pulled you over, they can "find" all kinds of things in your car. And in some cases, if they don't find what they want, they are not above planting it; like a little bag of coke placed under the passenger seat by one cop while another has you in the squad car answering questions. Not all cops, of course, do this, but it's a common enough occurrence to be worried about.

Even if the defendant is a drug dealer with a multi-page rap sheet; even if his harm to the community is palpable and real; even if the police, the prosecutors, and the courts are all convinced beyond a reasonable doubt that there was a bag of cocaine somewhere in the car; if the evidence was not obtained in accordance with the Constitution; if the police did not have a lawful basis for stopping and searching the car; if the police *broke* the law in order to *enforce* it, then the evidence of criminality must be excluded. If the police can mow down the Constitution to nail the Devil, they can mow it down to nail *anyone.* The history of human freedom is paying careful attention to the government's procedures.

I know I've wandered from the main question regarding my profound change of philosophy, heart, and general view of the legal world. I'm not avoiding it, exactly, so much as sneaking up on it gradually.

According to an old joke, "a conservative is a liberal who's been mugged, and a liberal is a conservative who's been arrested"; meaning, of course, that regardless of your beliefs in the abstract, one's personal experience tends to awaken one to reality, however unpleasant it may be.

Well, that's very much what happened to me. As a judge, I heard the police lie and lie again. I remember one case in which a driver had been pulled over and directed to walk away from the car by one cop, while his partner secretly kicked in the car's tail light. Why? To give the police a legal reason for the pull-over should it come up in court; which it did, of course.

The first time you encounter behavior of this sort on the part of men and women who carry badges and guns and swear to uphold the Constitution ("I do solemnly swear that I will support and defend the Constitution . . .") and swear to tell the truth (". . . the whole truth and nothing but the truth . . ."), and then do neither, something inside you just dies. To someone of my blue-collar, lower middle-class, Roman Catholic, respect-for-authority background, it was simply inconceivable.

You tell yourself that maybe it's just one cop. But then it happens again and again. As you gain more experience, you find police not only lying under oath, but using forced confessions and prosecutors withholding evidence helpful to a defendant, all in an effort to bring about convictions.

And then a cop I knew well came before me and lied. It was about a cocaine bust. I knew him so well I could tell he was lying to my face under oath when he told me the implausible reason about why he pulled over a known drug dealer and then just happened to find the cocaine on the front seat of this experienced drug dealer's car. My friend knows better than to admit that he lied. He broke the law by lying under oath (why wasn't *he* prosecuted for perjury?), and because of that a guilty defendant walks free; but from the police officer's view, they got the junk off the street (the minor amount they seized), and so he and his fellow police officers view this as a "win"—even though they broke the law.

CONSTITUTIONAL CHAOS

For eight years I was a judge of the Superior Court of New Jersey. I tried over one hundred fifty jury trials: murders, rapes, robberies, medical malpractice, antitrust, personal injury. I sentenced over a thousand people. I handled many thousands of motions, hearings, and divorces. I was a professor of law at Delaware Law School (now Widener Law School) and taught constitutional law and criminal procedure for one and a half years there, and I taught constitutional law as an adjunct professor at Seton Hall Law School for eleven years.

I am no longer a sitting judge or law school professor. But what I saw and studied and strained over taught me to speak with authority. I saw the beginnings—in my lifetime—of constitutional chaos.

The effect of my professional intimacy with the system was a sea change in my thinking. I can't point to any single moment of sudden and divine clarity. Instead, seeing, studying, and examining the events described in this book day after day eventually caused me to rethink the verities that had been literally a part of my soul since I matured into a thinking, adult human being.

The one incontrovertible lesson I learned over those hard, disillusioning years: Unless you work for it, sell to it, or receive financial assistance from it, *the government is not your friend.*

PART 3

THE HARD TEST:
THE WAR
ON TERROR

10

THE JUSTICE DEPARTMENT'S TERROR TACTICS

In response to the terrorist attacks on September 11th 2001, the U.S. government rounded up thousands of law-abiding immigrants and held them incommunicado for many months. Most were prosecuted in secret for technical INS violations. None was charged with terrorist activities.

The government did, of course, charge at least twenty people, some Americans, some aliens, with providing *material support* to terrorists. And in a unique and precedent-setting mode, it also charged some of their lawyers for getting too close to them.

HAMMERING LAWYERS

An assault on some of the terrorists' lawyers is the federal government's latest abusive and unconstitutional plan. Congress and the Justice Department have implemented tools that allow federal officials to interfere with a lawyer's ability to provide competent legal advice to his client. The government's latest effort at making it a crime for an attorney to represent zealously a client accused of terrorist acts is completely inconsistent with the constitutional principles contained in the First and Sixth Amendments, which guarantee the right of free speech and right to counsel, respectively. It is a direct challenge to the Constitution that the government has gone as far as prosecuting lawyers for *doing their jobs.*

Lynne Stewart is a sixty-four-year-old New York City criminal defense attorney, who has bravely defended some notorious defendants—frequently left-wing radicals—in recent years. Because Stewart represents those individuals whom the government most hates, the government decided that attorneys like her presented a danger to the government's efforts in the war on terror. While Stewart has taken an oath to counsel her clients to the best of her abilities, the government has made it a crime for her to show up at work. For doing just that, she now faces up to twenty years in federal prison.

Stewart represents Sheikh Omar Abdel Rahman, who is not exactly a sympathetic character. The "blind sheikh" masterminded the 1993 bombing of the World Trade Center and plotted to blow up other New York City landmarks. Sheikh Abdel Rahman is a leader of the Islamic Group, an Egyptian terrorist organization. Convicted in January 1996, Sheikh Abdel Rahman was sentenced to life imprisonment. On May 19, 2000, when Stewart sought to visit him in a federal prison, prison officials required her to sign an affirmation that she would abide by their Special Administrative Measures (SAMs). The SAMs required that Stewart "only be accompanied by translators for the purpose of communicating with [Sheikh Abdel Rahman] concerning legal matters" and that she would not use the meeting to "pass messages between third parties . . . and Abdel Rahman."

If the federal government had followed the law, Stewart would never have been required to agree to the SAMs. On October 31, 2001, Attorney General Ashcroft *secretly gave himself the power* to bypass the attorney-client privilege and eavesdrop on "confidential" conversations between prisoners and their attorneys. The regulation authorizing him to do so became effective immediately—without opportunity for public comment—so that Attorney General Ashcroft could unilaterally violate the attorney-client privilege if he had "reasonable suspicion . . . [to] believe that a particular inmate may use communications with attorneys or their agents to further or facilitate acts of violence or terrorism."

It is unbelievable that Attorney General Ashcroft purported to give himself the power to *suspend the Constitution*, whose Sixth Amendment guarantees an individual the right to consult with a lawyer in confidence. Attorney General Ashcroft's duty is to enforce the law, not re-write it. Not even Congress can suspend the attorney-client privilege. And, in addition to the Sixth Amendment guarantee, the attorney-client privilege is guaranteed in all fifty states. Thus, Attorney General Ashcroft has no power to usurp power from the state governments and declare that their laws are no longer valid. Had Attorney General Ashcroft followed the law he swore to uphold, Stewart would never have been required to agree to comply with the SAMs. This is crucial background information for understanding what followed.

During the prison visit, which the federal government tape-recorded, Sheikh Abdel Rahman and an Arabic translator who accompanied Stewart discussed whether the Islamic group should abandon a two-year-old "cease-fire" not to engage in further acts of terrorism. The government alleges that Stewart continuously made extraneous "gibberish" comments in English, in order to mask the Arabic conversation from the prison officials. After the meeting, Stewart issued a press release to the Reuters news service in order to help Sheikh Abdel Rahman communicate to the world his recommendation that the Islamic Group abandon the cease-fire.

That's the case against her: gibberish speech in jail and issuing a press release afterward.

In 2002, the Department of Justice caused a grand jury to indict Stewart. The charges included providing "material support" to a terrorist group, and committing "fraud" and making "false statements" in agreeing to abide by the SAMs. The two "material support" counts were so absurd that the federal judge in New York assigned to her case, Judge John Koeltl, dismissed them because they were unconstitutionally vague. The government's tortuous argument was that Stewart provided the Islamic Group with "personnel" and "communications equipment." But the "personnel" Stewart provided was not a single terrorist, but herself!

And the government claimed that providing the Islamic Group with "communications equipment" consisted of using a computer to type up the Reuters news release. Judge Koeltl rejected this argument because Stewart wasn't even accused of turning over any people or equipment to the terrorist group. Does a newspaper that quotes terrorists' demands provide them with communications equipment?

After this defeat, the government refiled the charges and invoked a different provision of the "material support" statute. This time, the legal theory was that Sheikh Abdel Rahman was Stewart's "personnel," and Stewart knowingly provided "material support" to him. Under this theory, the government claims that it was Stewart's intent to give assistance to members of a terrorist conspiracy headed by her client. Stewart says her only intent was to represent her client, and her principal professional duty was to give assistance to a convicted terrorist—her client!

The government's prosecution of Stewart demonstrates a complete contempt for the Sixth Amendment right to counsel and the First Amendment right to free speech. Stewart's duty, in a controversial case, is to advocate for her client in the press, just as the government uses the press to advocate against defendants it indicts. The government is trying to make it a crime for Stewart to represent her client's interests. In doing so, the government is violating Sheikh Abdel Rahman's constitutional right to counsel: Stewart can't effectively represent her client if the government listens to and records their privileged conversations and if the threat of a government prosecution is looming during the attorney-client meeting. Thus, zealous representation is impossible if an attorney's first concern is avoiding her own prosecution. Additionally, Stewart's constitutional right to free speech prevents the government from prosecuting her on the basis of a *statement* she made to the media. Her right to free speech allows her to decide whether to help her client communicate with the outside world. Furthermore, Stewart never advocated acts of terrorism; she merely informed the media of a truthful statement by another individual: that Sheikh Abdel Rahman had decided to abandon the "cease-fire."

The "fraud" and "false statement" charges are just as ludicrous. The government's "fraud" case alleges that, when Stewart had signed the SAMs, she had no intention of abiding by the restrictions.

How can the government possibly prove that Stewart had such a state of mind? She could have signed the SAMs in good-faith and later decided not to conform to them. And the "false statement" count—accusing Stewart of lying when she agreed that she would not use her meetings with Sheikh Abdel Rahman to pass messages between him and third parties— is a constitutional outrage. Under a federal statute that makes it a crime to lie (not commit perjury by lying under oath) to a government official, a defense attorney can be prosecuted for lying to the government about her client's case. However, a prosecutor can lie to the defense attorney to his heart's content.

In a 1995 Supreme Court case, *Hubbard v. United States*, the Court expressed the principle that partisan prosecutors should not be empowered to take action against a lawyer directly for merely representing a client. As Justice Antonin Scalia explained, allowing the federal prosecutor to threaten the defendant's *lawyer* with imprisonment "will deter vigorous representation of opposing interests in adversarial litigation, particularly [when the federal government] control[s] the machinery" to prosecute a lawyer under the false statement statute.

The federal government is targeting Lynne Stewart because it wants to intimidate defense attorneys either to refuse to represent accused terrorists or to provide less than zealous representation for fear of imprisonment. As Stewart stated at the time of her arrest, "They've arrested the lawyer and the interpreter. How much further are they going to go? Are they going to arrest the lady that cleans the sheikh's cell [because she provided him with material assistance]?"

The federal government's post-September 11th assault on lawyers who defend terrorists not only includes prosecution for providing legal counsel but also includes accusations of actually *being* a terrorist. The government's message is clear: If you defend someone we say is a terrorist, we may declare you to be one of them and deprive you of all your freedoms!

TARGETED FOR HIS FAITH

Brandon Mayfield is an attorney and an American citizen, born in Ohio and raised in Kansas. He is married to an Egyptian-born woman and is also a Muslim convert. When Jeffrey Battle, one of the members of the "Portland Seven," a suspected terror cell in Oregon, was arrested in Fall 2002, Mayfield represented Battle in a custody dispute involving Battle's six-year-old daughter. Mayfield didn't represent any of the "Portland Seven" in the terrorism prosecutions.

The government thought it could put Mayfield behind bars because he is a Muslim and had advised Battle. On March 11, 2004, a vicious Al Qaeda-linked bombing in Madrid, Spain, caused 191 deaths and an additional 2,000 injuries. Mayfield was arrested on May 6, 2004, as a "material witness" in connection with the bombings. The FBI executed search warrants and raided his home and law firm.

The FBI alleged that a fingerprint was found from one of Mayfield's fingers on a plastic bag retrieved from the wreckage of the bombing. Federal government agents told a federal judge that the fingerprint was a 100 percent match and that they were "absolutely certain" it belonged to Mayfield.

Spanish authorities had doubts about the fingerprint identification and continued to analyze it. The Spanish authorities cautioned the FBI against falsely accusing Mayfield of being responsible for the bombings, but the FBI refused these warnings and went ahead with the arrest. Local authorities reminded their American colleagues that they examined the original print, but FBI experts only saw a facsimile version. And, for what it's worth, Mayfield told the FBI he had never traveled to Spain.

Disturbingly, the federal government's affidavit used to secure Mayfield's arrest warrant painted him as a Muslim extremist. It stressed

Mayfield's Muslim *faith*, his *marriage* to an Egyptian-born woman, and the fact that he *represented* a terrorist in a child custody battle. Look at the emphasized words in the previous sentence. Your government and mine persuaded a federal judge to authorize Mayfield's arrest because of his faith (protected by the First Amendment), his marriage (protected by Supreme Court cases and state statutes), and his choice of clients (for the exercise of which he has a valid state-issued license).

After Mayfield spent fourteen days in jail, the FBI admitted that the print was "of no value for identification purposes." The FBI's mistake was so egregious that it took the rare step of publicly apologizing to Mayfield. But despite its *faux pas*, the FBI still refused to clear Mayfield even after his release from prison. Until a federal judge dismissed the material witness complaint, Mayfield remained classified as a "material witness" and had restrictions placed on his movements.

Numerous questions remain about the federal government's attack on Mayfield. In Mayfield's words, a 100 percent fingerprint match is "a death sentence." It is unfathomable that the government could be "absolutely certain," yet so wrong, with regard to something of that magnitude, especially given the warning from the Spanish authorities. A high-ranking Spanish National Police official opined on the FBI witch hunt against Mayfield: "It seemed as though they had something against him . . . and they wanted to involve us."

The only thing that is clear is that the federal government sought to stop another lawyer—who represented a client in a matrimonial case long before the client was accused of terrorist acts—from going about his professional life and from being free.

SECRECY IN THE COURTROOM

In addition to its assault on lawyers, the post-September 11th federal government has implemented a complete attack on the right of the public and the media to observe trials. The constitutional right to free speech triggers the right to listen. Accordingly, the Constitution guarantees that the public can access any and all court proceedings, except (according to some courts) in cases involving physical harm to children. Yet, the federal government has started conducting deportation hearings in secret, despite the public's First Amendment right of access.

Rabih Haddad, a native of Lebanon, was taken into INS custody in December 2001 for overstaying his six-month tourist visa. After holding Haddad in jail for a year, the government initiated removal proceedings and held a hearing on December 19, 2002. Haddad's family, members of the public, and newspaper reporters were in the courtroom, planning to observe the trial. However, shortly before the trial was to begin, courtroom officials announced that it was closed to the press and public. Neither Haddad nor his attorney had prior notice of the closure and objected. The immigration judge announced that the decision came from her supervisors, and that she lacked the power to reverse the decision. What followed is anyone's guess.

In 1988, Malek Zeidan, a forty-two-year-old native of Syria, came to the United States on a six-month tourist visa. He decided not to leave and spent the next fourteen years creating a successful canary breeding business. On January 31, 2002, an INS agent appeared at his door, whereupon Zeidan was arrested for the visa violation. He was turned over to INS custody, and a deportation hearing was scheduled for February 21, 2002.

Members of the public and two newspaper reporters were sitting in the courtroom when Zeidan's case was called. The immigration judge asked the government attorney whether the matter was a "special interest" case, and the attorney responded in the affirmative. Subsequently, the judge ordered all members of the public and media to leave the courtroom. As in the Haddad case, what happened to Zeidan is unknown.

When the federal government decrees a "special interest" case and then escorts the public out of the courtroom, it smacks of Stalinism.

MAKING SUSPECTS DISAPPEAR

Attorney General John Ashcroft's latest courtroom policy doesn't fall far from that. Ten days after the terrorist attacks of September 11th 2001, Attorney General Ashcroft sent a memorandum to all immigration judges (these "judges" are actually employees of the Justice Department) that the attorney general has "implemented additional security procedures for certain cases in the Immigration Court." These "special interest" cases trigger "additional security" procedures, meaning that judges must, among other things, "close the hearing[s] to the public." The memorandum further decrees "no visitors, no family, no press."

Once Attorney General Ashcroft selects a case to be of "special interest," his decision is final. There is no individualized determination requiring the government to demonstrate that *the public trial itself* presents a national security risk. Neither the immigration judge nor the immigrant's attorney can challenge Attorney General Ashcroft's determination.

As if all this wasn't enough, Attorney General Ashcroft stripped the public of our access to the immigration court's *docket* itself. As such, the immigration court is prohibited from confirming or denying whether a particular individual's case is listed for trial or, if so, if it is deemed of "special interest."

Essentially, once Attorney General Ashcroft makes that designation, that person disappears. Not even the immigrant's family is able to find out what happened to the person, even after that person has been deported. Josef Stalin also had a way of making people disappear; he would often purge a particular individual's name and image from every record, printing, or photograph in which it appeared, and forbid those in his government from talking about the person.

WHY PUBLIC ACCESS MATTERS

Outraged after being shunned out of the immigration courtroom during Rabih Haddad's hearing, some media companies sued the federal government in a federal district court in Michigan. The trial judge found the government's secrecy policy unconstitutional and granted an injunction against the secret dockets and trials, thereby prohibiting the government from restricting the press's and the public's First Amendment right of access.

On August 26, 2002, the U.S. Court of Appeals for the Sixth Circuit unanimously affirmed the trial court's ruling that the federal government's secrecy policy was unconstitutional. In this case, *Detroit Free Press v. Ashcroft*, Judge Damon Keith strongly condemned the government: "Democracies die behind closed doors. . . . When the government begins closing doors, it selectively controls information rightfully belonging to the people. Selective information is misinformation."

Judge Keith, while recognizing that national security sometimes requires secrecy, criticized the blanket process of allowing Attorney General Ashcroft to act as judge, jury, and executioner in designating "special interest" cases. Because the process is "performed in secret, without any established standards or procedures, . . . not subject to any sort of review by . . . the courts," there exists "no real safeguard on this exercise of authority."

Judge Keith wrote that the federal government should have made determinations on whether to restrict public access to the courtroom on a case-by-case basis, evaluating the potential national security threat of *each individual.* Additionally, the court held that the government had no good reason for prohibiting the deportee and the public from even *challenging* the attorney general's decision to close the courtroom.

Expressing fear that the government "could operate in virtual secrecy . . . by simple assertion of 'national security,'" Judge Keith warned that under Attorney General Ashcroft's edict there is "no limit" to the government's possible "wholesale suspension of First Amendment rights."

Furthermore, he noted numerous reasons why the public's right to access these immigration cases is essential to our free society. For one, public access serves as a check on the government's actions "by assuring us that proceedings are conducted fairly and properly" and that "the government does its job properly [and] does not make mistakes." Additionally, having an open courtroom "enhances the perception of integrity and fairness" and gives "legitimacy" to the government's actions. The individual citizen's right to participate in "our republican system of self-government" is also important because an informed public can seek redress against a government that acted inappropriately.

FIRST AMENDMENT LOSS

Just as Judge Keith found it abundantly clear that Attorney General Ashcroft's secrecy policy was unconstitutional, so did a federal trial judge in Newark, New Jersey, Judge John Bissell, who reviewed the government's decision to bar the press and public from Malek Zeidan's hearing.

The government appealed *New Jersey Media Group v. Ashcroft* to the U.S. Court of Appeals for the Third Circuit. Disturbingly, that court's two-to-one majority decided to look the other way in the face of the federal government's assault on the First Amendment. That court ruled that the attorney general has a free pass to violate the First Amendment at his choosing, "in recognition of [Attorney General Ashcroft's] experience (and our lack of experience) in this field, we will defer to his judgment."

This ruling was premised on the fallacious argument that immigration hearings aren't traditionally open to the public (like a criminal trial would be), a contention that Judge Keith had already debunked. In response to the fact that there is no judicial remedy available for these closures, the court found it sufficient that citizens unsatisfied with Attorney General Ashcroft could vote the president out of office four years later and look forward to another attorney general!

As a result of this ruling, the First Amendment right to view federal immigration trials in Delaware, New Jersey, Pennsylvania, and the Virgin Islands (the states which constitute the Third Circuit), only applies when the attorney general wants it to apply.

Despite the enormous magnitude of this case, the U.S. Supreme Court refused to review the Third Circuit's deviation from Judge Keith's Sixth Circuit opinion. In the Third Circuit states, the Constitution's guarantee of free speech now means whatever Attorney General Ashcroft says it means in light of the war on terror.

BYE-BYE, FOURTH AMENDMENT

Post-September 11th attacks on the Constitution do not stop at the First Amendment's free speech guarantee. Also under attack is the Fourth Amendment's protection against unreasonable searches and seizures, which provides that "no warrants shall issue but on probable cause, supported by an oath or affirmation, and particularly describing the place to be searched, and the persons or things to be seized."

In his famous dissent in *Olmstead v. United States*, Justice Brandeis called privacy—which he defined as "the right to be let alone"—"the most comprehensive of rights and the right most valued by civilized men." Apparently many current members of Congress and the Justice Department, all of whom have sworn to uphold the Constitution, and thus, the right to privacy, disagree since they have continued our slow, inexorable march toward the erosion of this most basic right.

The Constitution prohibits invasions of privacy by the government by denying it the power to engage in unreasonable searches and seizures absent a warrant issued upon probable cause. Probable cause hinges on having an amount of evidence sufficient to induce the belief in the mind of a neutral judge that the target of the search more likely than not has committed or is committing a crime. Without enough evidence for probable cause, the government must respect our right to be let alone.

An individual's right to be let alone has, for centuries, been a quintessential hallmark of a free society.

An English case, decided in 1603, recognized the right of a homeowner to defend against unlawful entry even by agents of the King: "Every man's house is his castle." But, under King George III's tyrannical rule over the colonies, the right to be let alone began to evaporate.

In the early 1760s, Parliament authorized British customs officials to use "writs of assistance" in order to apprehend colonists who were suspected of smuggling goods. If a British customs official wanted to break into a colonist's house, he merely needed to draft a search warrant (then known as a writ of assistance) and *sign it himself*! Furthermore, the writ of assistance was valid to search all of the colonist's possessions and was good until King George III died.

James Otis, a colonial attorney, first expressed the outrage felt by the colonists over these writs of assistance. In 1761, he warned against such "a power that places the liberty of every man in the hands of every petty officer." The Founding Fathers incorporated this sentiment into the Bill of Rights, as the Fourth Amendment prohibits writs of assistance and establishes standards for searches and seizures.

And from the adoption of the Bill of Rights on December 15, 1791, until October 26, 2001, we could actually enjoy this right to be left alone.

Before October of 2001, if the government wanted documents about you which were in the possession of a third person, a financial institution for example, it could either present probable cause under oath to a federal judge or to a grand jury that was investigating you. If the judge agreed, or if the grand jury agreed, the warrant or subpoena was authorized, a record was made of the probable cause, and the warrant or subpoena was then served on the custodian of the records.

The custodian, in turn, would inform you of the documents sought and thus give you time to contest the warrant or subpoena before a judge. If your contest was successful—perhaps you showed a judge that a government clerk misidentified a bank account number and it wasn't really your banking records the government wanted—then the warrant or subpoena would be quashed and you and your personal documents would be safe from the government's eyes. If the government prevailed—say, it made out a probable cause case of tax evasion against you to the judge before whom you filed your challenge—the custodian would be directed to turn over the documents and the government would continue to build its case against you.

In either case, the rights guaranteed to you by the Fourth Amendment would have been honored because a neutral judge would have examined and scrutinized the government's behavior. Win or lose, the government got to make its case and you had the opportunity to resist and defend.

Unfortunately, all this has slowly changed. Since 1977, the Justice Department and various intelligence agencies of the government have had the power to issue—without immediate judicial intervention—administrative subpoenas which require custodians of records in industries regulated by the government, like financial institutions, to surrender documents about people involved in national security. The target is supposed to be a foreign agent, even of a friendly government.

The idea behind the grant of this power was that our intelligence agencies need to know who may be spying on us, whether friend or foe. If a foreign "journalist" is really a spy, and we could ascertain that, we wouldn't, and we couldn't, prosecute him because the evidence against him was obtained without probable cause, thus in violation of the Constitution, but we could kick him out of the country.

Our intelligence agencies, like the CIA, were forbidden to share what they found with prosecuting agencies, like the FBI, and if prosecutors stumbled on this stuff, they could not use it, because it was obtained without probable cause, and thus was constitutionally incompetent as evidence in a criminal case.

On October 26, 2001, the so-called USA PATRIOT Act changed all this. In addition to numerous other violations of the Constitution which it purports to sanction, it specifically authorizes intelligence agencies to give what they obtain without probable cause to prosecutors, and it authorizes prosecutors to use the information thus received in ordinary criminal prosecutions.

And to make matters worse, the custodians of the records are now prohibited from *telling* you that your records were sought or surrendered. So much for "Congress shall make no law abridging . . . the freedom of speech. . . ."

This is more than just academic. If the government can get documents about you and evidence against you from your financial institution under the guise of national security, i.e., without a showing of probable cause, but use it in a criminal case against you, then the Constitution's protections—its guarantees—have been eviscerated. Without fidelity to the Constitution, there is no privacy, and without privacy there is nothing to prevent the government from breaking down doors in the night—under the guise of national security—and taking whatever or whomever it wants.

WRITS REBORN

As if all of this were not enough constitutional mischief from this government, the Congress recently engaged in some truly Orwellian newspeak in order to broaden the scope of administrative subpoenas.

On Saturday afternoon, December 13, 2003, the right to privacy suffered another serious blow. On that day, the day he learned that Saddam Hussein had been captured, President Bush signed into law the Intelligence Authorization Act for fiscal year 2004. This statute expands the term "financial institution" so as to now include travel agencies and car dealers, casinos and their hotels, real estate and insurance agents and lawyers, newsstands and pawnbrokers, and even the Post Office!

Now, without you knowing it, the Justice Department—whose lawyers and agents have sworn to uphold the Constitution—can easily subvert it by learning where you traveled, what you spent, who you slept with, what you ate, what you paid to finance your car and your house, what you confided to your lawyer and insurance and real estate agents, and what periodicals you read without having to demonstrate any evidence or even suspicion of criminal activity on your part. *And the government can now, for the first time in American history, without obtaining the approval of a court, read your mail before you do, and prosecute you on the basis of what it reads!*

Have we gone back to the colonial period and the tyrannical rule of King George III? It sure sounds like the federal government has brought back those writs of assistance which the Constitution has banned for over two hundred years.

There's an ironic twist to this: If the government does not prosecute you, you'll never know the extent to which it has invaded your privacy!

SNOOPING SUFFOCATES FREEDOM

None of this was supposed to have happened. The tools Congress gave to intelligence agencies are only constitutional when used just for intelligence purposes—like watching or deporting foreign spies—and only against genuine foreign threats. When criminal prosecution is implicated, the Constitution's protections are triggered.

Most Americans don't want the government to know of their personal behavior; not because we have anything to hide, but because we don't live in the former East Germany or the old Soviet Union; because government in a free society is supposed to serve the people, not spy on them; because without probable cause, without some demonstrable evidence of some personal criminal behavior, the Constitution declares that our personal lives are none of the federal government's business.

Government is not reason or eloquence, George Washington once said, it is force. That's why we have a Constitution: to restrain the government's exercise of force so we can be a free people.

Government surveillance undermines freedom because it is natural to hesitate to exercise freedom when the government is watching and recording. Numerous Supreme Court decisions have underscored this by holding that freedom needs breathing room. With the government's snooping nose and undisciplined eyes in our hotel rooms, lawyers' offices, and mailboxes, few will have the courage to be free; and freedom will suffocate.

Has the government that we voted into power forgotten that we value more than just safety and security? The Declaration of Independence defines the whole purpose of the American enterprise as guarantees of life, liberty, and the pursuit of happiness. How can we be free and happy with the government watching nearly everything we do?

Justice Brandeis argued that the framers knew that Americans wanted protection from intrusion by the government not only for our property but also for our thoughts, ideas, and emotions. In its prosecution of the war on terror, the government says it is defending the homeland. But if it does not defend our values, if it actually attacks our basic rights like privacy, what is it really defending?

RIGHTS NO MORE

In July 2003, the U.S. Department of Justice held a celebration at which it handed out honors and praises to the federal agents and lawyers involved in the prosecution of the Lackawanna Six.

It should have handed out indictments instead, because those prosecutors—or at least some of them—violated their oaths to uphold the Constitution in order to coerce six soccer-playing young men from Lackawanna, New York, with no criminal records, into accepting long jail terms, well out of proportion to their alleged crimes.

The six—all Arab-Americans in their early twenties, five of whom were born here—were charged in federal court in the Western District of New York with providing aid and support to a terrorist group, before September 11th, by attending camps in Afghanistan and *listening* to Muslim clerics preach hatred at the United States.

They were not charged with waging war against the United States, like John Walker Lindh. They were not arrested in the midst of a battlefield, like the sixty prisoners of war we recently released from Guantanamo Bay. They were not charged with causing or planning harm.

They were charged with *listening* to others—including, in the case of one of them, Osama bin Laden himself—talk about causing America harm. The government actually told a federal judge that since the clerics being *heard* by the six were terrorists, the six had committed crimes of violence.

The court rejected that argument out of hand. After reviewing the evidence against the six, the judge wrote that these defendants—like all defendants—are guaranteed due process, and that federal courts should do more than just pay lip service to the guarantees of the Declaration of Independence and the Constitution, they should enforce them.

"We must never adopt an 'end justifies the means' philosophy," the judge wrote, "by claiming that our Constitutional and democratic principles must be temporarily furloughed or put on hold in cases involving alleged terrorism in order to preserve our democracy. To do so would result in victory for the terrorists."

But within mere yards of where this fair judge sat when he wrote those words, the government lawyers who once swore to uphold the Constitution were plotting to put it on hold.

According to a lawyer for one of the six—himself a former federal prosecutor—the government lawyers implicitly threatened the six during plea negotiations that if they did not plead guilty, if they did not speak up as the government wished, if they did not cooperate in their own prosecutions, if they insisted on their due process rights, the government would declare them to be enemy combatants.

In that case, these so-called defenders of the Constitution threatened, the six would have no due process rights, no trial, no lawyers, no charges filed against them, and they would receive solitary confinement for life.

Could the government actually do this? How can defendants be stripped of all their rights *before* conviction? Aren't rights guaranteed, no matter how aggressive the prosecution or odious the defendants?

There is no reported case in American history in which a court allowed a defendant to be told that his insistence on due process would result not in prosecution and conviction, but in punishment without trial. It has always been the case that when entering a guilty plea—and when negotiating for that plea—the defendant's fears of punishment were limited to that which the law provides. Today, for the government to threaten that the punishment can be increased by fiat by the president after the crime has been committed is not only unconstitutional, it is tyrannical.

LIBERTY: VOID WHERE PROHIBITED

It is only a warped view of American history, culture, and law that could seriously suggest constitutional rights are discretionary—that any president can strip any person of his due process rights. Let's be clear: There is no Supreme Court case supporting or authorizing presidential enhancement of punishment, and the Justice Department knows that.

So why then did the lawyers for the Lackawanna Six let their clients plead guilty and accept six-to-nine-year jail terms for the crime of *listening* to anti-American rants in the face of a threat to do the constitutionally impossible? Because they knew that the government has suspended rights before and has gotten away with it. They knew that the president had actually declared three people to be enemy combatants and had kept them locked up without charges and away from their own lawyers; and before the Supreme Court stepped in, he appeared to be getting away with it.

As children we were taught that tyranny can't happen here. Doesn't the Constitution guarantee rights to the worst among us, and didn't the president and his lawyers in the Justice Department swear an oath to uphold the Constitution? Not when it comes to national defense, the government has argued. But doesn't national defense mean defense of our values as well as our real estate? Not if the defendants are dangerous, according to this Justice Department. But isn't everyone who has been arrested—even a jaywalker—entitled to counsel? If the government doesn't file charges, it absurdly argues, the defendant doesn't need a lawyer.

This is more than absurd.

It is terrifying.

The American system of justice is the best and most equitable in the world because of its fidelity to the rule of law in which an independent judiciary enforces everyone's due process rights. But when prosecutors seek victory through illegal threats—rather than through fair negotiation or through the slow methodical presentation of evidence to a jury—they corrupt the cause they seek to advance.

The whole purpose of our adversarial system of criminal prosecutions is to assure that only those whose guilt the government proves beyond a reasonable doubt are punished. This is the rule of law. Anything short of that, any governmental triumph by private intimidation instead of public confrontation, is unwise, unfair, and un-American.

11

THROWING AWAY THE
JAIL HOUSE KEY

The government illegally seized three human beings and stripped them of all their guaranteed rights. They were placed under indefinite solitary confinement in a military jail and were allowed no visitors, except government interrogators. No charges were filed against them. They were never brought to trial. They were never convicted of a crime. They never appeared before a judge. Their jailors have barred them from speaking to a lawyer. There is little possibility that their rights will be returned to them.

Sounds like the old Soviet Union? Not quite.

Welcome to post-September 11th America, where the federal government has claimed for itself unlimited power to take any action necessary to achieve its goals in the war on terror, including the blatant destruction of Americans' basic guaranteed liberties.

MATERIAL WITNESS TYRANNY

Shortly after September 11th, federal officials decided that Chicago's O'Hare airport was a battlefield in the war on terror. On May 8, 2002, Jose Padilla, born in Brooklyn and raised in Chicago, had just landed at O'Hare from Pakistan. He was quietly grabbed and whisked away by FBI agents. No public announcement of the arrest was made, and it seemed that Padilla had just vanished.

Padilla was initially named as a material witness in the war on terror. Calling someone a "material witness" is a tactic that the federal government has begun implementing as a means of locking up people who it worries about but who have not committed any provable crime. The government has arrested, and indefinitely held, dozens of individuals under the federal material witness statute. The government gave itself the power to hold these "material witnesses" in solitary confinement, without charging them with any crimes and without even having probable cause that they committed any crimes.

One federal judge in New York found this practice patently unconstitutional. "Relying on the material witness statute to detain people who are presumed innocent under our Constitution in order to prevent potential crimes is illegitimate," Judge Shira Scheindlin ruled.

While a material witness can be temporarily detained in order to secure testimony *at a pending proceeding* if and when it is clear that the witness will not come to court voluntarily, the government has abused its authority because these "material witnesses" often aren't even alleged to have been *witnesses* to any particular crime, and there is frequently no pending grand jury proceeding or trial before which they had been summoned and refused to testify.

Despite Judge Scheindlin's finding that the government is using the "material witness" statute as a front for violating civil liberties, a court of appeals reversed her ruling and surrendered a small part of the judiciary's power to be an effective check on the executive branch.

The government is abusing and circumventing the material witness statute's legitimate purpose. If the government requires an individual—who witnessed a crime—to testify on the government's behalf at trial, and that individual is a flight risk, the government may arrest that person in order to ensure his appearance at trial.

The material witness statute has several protections: the government must prove that the individual is likely to flee, the judge must approve the arrest warrant, and the individual is entitled to a bail hearing. This detention is temporary and merely lasts for the duration of the trial before which the material witness has been subpoenaed to testify. As Judge Scheindlin noted, the government is forbidden from decreeing someone a material witness so that it can indefinitely hold that person until it convenes a grand jury and the grand jury's investigation is complete.

So, who had Padilla refused to testify about? No one; he wasn't even asked to testify. And the Fifth Amendment, of course, prevents the government from compelling any person to be a material witness *against himself.*

The government soon realized that there was no evidence sufficient to charge Padilla with any crime, and it acknowledged, not publicly, that he wasn't a government witness to anything. So the president, rather than release Padilla, decreed that Padilla was an "enemy combatant" and transferred him from Justice Department custody in New York to Defense Department custody in South Carolina.

On the day after Padilla was taken from the Metropolitan Correctional Center in lower Manhattan, U.S. Attorney General John Ashcroft, who was in Moscow at the time, rushed out in front of the Kremlin (got to love the irony of that) and held a live press conference at which he announced to the world that the government had "disrupted an unfolding terrorist plot to attack the United States."

Ashcroft claimed to have "captured a known terrorist who was exploring a plan to build and explode a radiological dispersion device, or 'dirty bomb,' in the United States." Ashcroft, who referred to Padilla by the name Abdullah Al Muhajir, went on to declare that "Muhajir is an enemy combatant who poses a serious and continuing threat to the American people and our national security." Where did he get the phrase "enemy combatant" from?

GETTING AROUND THE CONSTITUTION

The Department of Justice has yet to present to a court any direct evidence of Padilla's involvement in Al Qaeda or a terrorist plot to use a dirty bomb in the United States.

The day after the Ashcroft press conference in Moscow, the second highest-ranking official in the Department of Defense debunked the attorney general's claims and conceded that the government had no case against Padilla. Deputy Defense Secretary Paul Wolfowitz stated that the Defense Department didn't "think there was actually a [terrorist] plot beyond some fairly loose talk." From this we can conclude that even top members of the executive branch had been aware that their colleagues were violating the Constitution by stripping innocent persons of their guaranteed rights.

On September 18, 2001, Congress approved a joint resolution, the Authorization for Use of Military Force (AUMF), which authorized the president to use "all necessary and appropriate force" against Al Qaeda and other nations or organizations that "committed or aided in the September 11th attacks."

Wanting more than just the power to wage war, the government soon decided that AUMF meant that it is inconvenient to wage war when the Constitution gets in the way. What can the government do when it is unable to try and convict someone it fears? It can proclaim to itself the authority to hold the person indefinitely as an "enemy combatant." This amounts to tyranny and is exactly why the framers of the Constitution gave us a president rather than a king.

Padilla's detention, as an enemy combatant, is a circuitous and illegal means of taking away his constitutional rights. The government's argument goes like this: The Sixth Amendment guarantees a criminal defendant the right to legal counsel. But, that right is not triggered until charges have been filed. Since the government isn't required to file charges against an enemy combatant, and hasn't done so, Padilla is not entitled to meet with his lawyer.

The administration also contends that courts have no power to second-guess the president's decision to designate Padilla as an enemy combatant because the decision to do so was made by the president not in his capacity as chief executive, but in his capacity as commander-in-chief, an area of executive branch behavior traditionally immune from judicial review.

Two judges have told the president that he usurped Congress's authority and ruled that Padilla is entitled to meet with his lawyer and to have a hearing in civilian federal district court. However, the U.S. Court of Appeals for the Second Circuit reached the correct result for the wrong reasons.

The two-to-one majority held that the president had no power to declare Padilla an enemy combatant because *Congress had not authorized him to do so.* According to the majority, it would have upheld the president's action had Congress enacted a law giving the president complete and inherent authority to take away the constitutional rights of American citizens.

SUPREME BUNGLE

Padilla appealed to the U.S. Supreme Court. In June 2004, by a five-to-four majority, the court ignored the government's illegal detention of Padilla and dismissed the appeal on a procedural point. The court ruled that, because Padilla's attorney filed the *habeas corpus* application with the federal district court in New York two days after Padilla was moved from civilian custody there to military custody in South Carolina, the trial judge in New York had no jurisdiction to rule on the case. This narrow ruling rejected the argument that "fairness and efficiency" take priority over an absurdly narrow reading of the jurisdiction statute.

The Supreme Court justices ducked the due process issue and failed to adhere to their constitutional responsibility to protect Padilla's inalienable rights. Even more shocking, had the court properly found that Padilla's application was properly filed, a majority of the Court would have ruled that Padilla is entitled to challenge his detention. The four dissenting justices wrote that there is "only one possible answer to the question whether [Padilla] is entitled to a hearing on the justification for his detention." Furthermore, a fifth justice, Justice Antonin Scalia—one of the five justices who ruled that the federal district court in New York had no jurisdiction to hear Padilla's application—stated in a separate opinion on the same issue that the government cannot hold an American against his will without first filing criminal charges.

The court got it wrong. Don't the federal courts have jurisdiction over Padilla's jailer?

Just as the president cannot restrict a citizen's constitutional due process rights, neither can Congress take those rights away. Seventeenth-century philosopher John Locke famously articulated the notion that humans have natural rights that cannot be violated by any person, government, or society. This principle is deeply ingrained in American tradition, including the writings of our Founding Fathers, the Declaration of Independence, the Bill of Rights, and the Constitution.

Jose Padilla's natural and inalienable right to procedural due process—notice of charges, use of an attorney and the subpoena power, fair hearing before a neutral jury, and the right to appeal judicial errors—is *guaranteed* by the Constitution. He has the right to meet with his attorney, the presumption of innocence, the right to have charges brought against him, and the right to a speedy trial. As devastating as the events of September 11th 2001 were, no part of the federal government has any authority to deprive Padilla of these rights. These natural rights trump the will of our elected officials, and only Congress can suspend the right to *habeas corpus*—the right to judicial review of one's incarceration—in a time of invasion or rebellion. It has never done so.

BY ANY OTHER NAME

How did all this happen? It came about when Attorney General Ashcroft and others in the government basically invented the term "enemy combatant." Prior to the war on terror, the term appeared nowhere in U.S. criminal law, international law, or the laws of war. Additionally, there is no written definition, nor a statement by the government, of who can be considered an enemy combatant.

The Geneva Conventions apply to lawful combatants (prisoners of war) and unlawful combatants (individuals fighting for a group that is not a nation). The Department of Justice realized that Padilla—an American citizen arrested on U.S. soil—was neither, and thus could not be brought before a military tribunal under the Geneva Conventions. Accordingly, the government created the "enemy combatant" category as a means of avoiding the Constitution when individuals are not entitled to the protections of the Geneva Conventions. For an individual like Padilla, the "enemy combatant" category is simply an illegal means of stripping an American citizen of his guaranteed rights.

The government's justification for the "enemy combatant" classification comes from a shameful revision of recent American history.

It has relied on the curious 1942 U.S. Supreme Court case of *Ex parte Quirin* as the principal basis for its authority to declare someone an enemy combatant. In that case, a group of German soldiers—who smuggled their way into the U.S. and planned sabotage—challenged their convictions for crimes of war. The Supreme Court used the term "enemy combatant" as a throwaway term to describe the German soldiers, since, because they were arrested on U.S. soil out of uniform, they could not be considered prisoners of war. (The Geneva Conventions, and their predecessor treaties, require the wearing of a uniform or other visible recognizable insignia in order to trigger their protections.)

In using this precedent, the government completely ignored the fact that these German soldiers were charged, had lawyers, were prosecuted, were convicted, and were sentenced by a military tribunal! Even if such an "enemy combatant" category exists, the same Supreme Court ruling on which the government relies unambiguously gives Padilla the right to some form of a fair trial, at a minimum. The government simply invented the idea that it can hold citizens incommunicado for an indefinite amount of time and without access to counsel. Nowhere does *Quirin* even hint at such a suggestion, and no other post-Geneva Convention American government has ever claimed such powers for itself.

Padilla was also the victim of a federal trial judge failing to perform his constitutional function. Shortly after Padilla was declared an enemy combatant, Padilla's lawyer brought a *habeas corpus* petition on Padilla's behalf, arguing that Padilla had not been lawfully imprisoned. *Habeas corpus* is the right guaranteed by the Constitution to all prisoners to be brought before a neutral judge by the government official confining the prisoners and to demand legal justification for the confinement.

Judge Michael Mukasey, the federal district judge assigned to hear the Padilla application, caved in to the heightened fears of the American public and ruled that he had no constitutional problem with the president's self-proclaimed, king-like powers to win the war on terror. The judge upheld the government's right to grab American citizens on U.S. soil and hold them "for the duration of the hostilities." The "hostilities"—the global war on terror—may last for years or even decades; depending upon how it's defined, it may never end. Judge Mukasey's ruling allows the government to hold Padilla in a military brig, without trial, for the rest of his life. To echo Defense Secretary Donald Rumsfeld, the administration is "not interested in trying [Padilla] at the moment . . . not interested in punishing him at the moment." But "the moment" could outlast Padilla's natural life.

Not interested in trying him? Then return him to freedom!

The essence of Judge Mukasey's ruling was that the government need only to offer "some evidence" that Padilla is an enemy combatant. The judge set the bar so low that hearsay can be characterized as "some evidence." Hearsay ("I have been told that Padilla had evil plans.") is not permitted in American trials because it is inherently untrustworthy: it can be mere rumor or innuendo, and it cannot be cross-examined.

In Judge Mukasey's courtroom, the sole "evidence" against Padilla was a declaration from Pentagon special advisor Michael H. Mobbs, which was merely a regurgitation of facts *told to* Mr. Mobbs by Department of Justice and CIA agents: classic hearsay.

Judge Mukasey also ruled that courts have no power to second-guess the president's decision to declare someone to be an enemy combatant. So, the incredibly weak "some evidence" standard ultimately becomes a "no evidence" standard. Rather than weighing the evidence and allowing the victim of the government's lawlessness to challenge the government's assertions, the court simply accepted the Mobbs Declaration at face value.

This is a refusal to perform the judicial function. Courts *must* second-guess the executive branch, because the government cannot be trusted to examine its own behavior. After arguing before the highest court in the land that Padilla was so dangerous that he could not be trusted alone in a jail cell in a military prison with his lawyers, the administration recently conceded that the claim that Padilla was making a "dirty bomb" was *wrong* and most likely can never be used in court against Padilla. Additionally, the administration withheld information from the courts which suggested that Al Qaeda was "very skeptical" about the success of the proposed dirty-bomb plot. Apparently, Attorney General Ashcroft's claim that the government had "disrupted an unfolding terrorist plot" was a scam and illustrates the need for checks on the authority of the executive branch.

In what was hailed as a "victory" for Padilla, Judge Mukasey did rule that Padilla was entitled to talk to a lawyer. But Judge Mukasey found that the Sixth Amendment's right to counsel did not apply to Padilla. Claiming that Padilla could use his lawyer as a conduit to send messages back to Al Qaeda, the Justice Department had barred Padilla from meeting with his attorney.

Judge Mukasey ordered the government to allow Padilla and his lawyer to discuss *only* the *habeas corpus* petition, and not even how he was being treated. The Justice Department resisted Judge Mukasey's order for one and a half years, but in March 2004, Padilla was finally allowed to meet with his attorney—even then, only in the presence of military handlers. In the words of Donna Newman, Padilla's chief attorney,

"They're throwing us a bone, as if we should be thrilled that they can now listen to our attorney-client conversations after my client's been held incommunicado, based on their say-so, for over a year and a half."

RIGHTS IN WARTIME

The Constitution is based on a system of checks and balances between the three branches of government. The system collapses when a court neglects its duty to second-guess the executive branch.

Even in wartime, the courts must ensure that the president does not abuse his constitutional authority. The Supreme Court made this explicitly clear in 1866 in the Civil War-era case of *Ex parte Merryman*, ruling that President Abraham Lincoln had violated the Constitution's Due Process Clause when he suspended the writ of *habeas corpus* in order to have Union officers arrest and indefinitely detain suspected secessionists.

In another Civil War case, *Ex parte Milligan*, the Supreme Court emphatically denied the president's authority to ignore the Constitution and try American civilians in military tribunals during wartime. Justice Davis wrote that "the Constitution of the United States is a law for rulers and people, equally in war and in peace, and covers with the shield of its protection all classes of men, at all times, and under all circumstances." Even during the Civil War era, federal courts had no difficulty enforcing the Constitution and restraining the president. Why are they reticent to do so now?

Jose Padilla's indefinite incommunicado detention is not an isolated incident. Since late 2001, Yasir Esam Hamdi has been locked away in the same Navy brig as Padilla in South Carolina. Like Padilla, Hamdi has not been charged or convicted of any crime, and he has repeatedly been denied the right to legal counsel. Also, like Padilla, Hamdi is an American. He was born in Baton Rouge, Louisiana, and raised in Saudi Arabia.

In late 2001, Hamdi was captured by Northern Alliance troops on the battlefield in Afghanistan. The U.S. government declared him an enemy combatant and sent him to Camp Delta at the American naval base at Guantanamo Bay, Cuba. After determining that he was probably an American citizen, the government transferred Hamdi to the South Carolina Navy brig.

A federal public defender, Frank Dunham, who read an article about Hamdi's indefinite detention, filed an application for *habeas corpus* relief on Hamdi's behalf, and U.S. District Judge Robert Doumar ordered the government to allow Hamdi to consult with his lawyer, but the government refused to obey the order.

A two-page hearsay declaration, again written by Pentagon special advisor Michael Mobbs, is the sole piece of "evidence" the government presented to the court to support the detention of Hamdi. This Mobbs Declaration—just like the one submitted in the Padilla case—merely recites allegations that were conveyed to Mobbs. Hamdi is said to have been "affiliated with a Taliban military unit and received weapons training" when he was captured in Afghanistan.

Judge Doumar ruled that the government did not present enough evidence to establish that Hamdi was an enemy or was engaged in combat with the United States. His opinion stated that the Mobbs Declaration was filled with "sparse facts" and "leads to more questions than answers." This courageous federal judge fulfilled his proper role in our system of an independent judiciary, announcing that he will not simply "rubber-stamp" the administration's assertions.

The judge properly concluded that the government never demonstrated Hamdi was a Taliban fighter, or even that Hamdi was a *member* of the Taliban. The government had never even alleged that Hamdi fired a weapon! Hamdi's attorneys personally told me that the government could not find a single witness to say that Hamdi ever used a weapon against Americans.

Despite Judge Doumar's findings that the government failed to establish that it had the authority to declare anyone an enemy combatant, failed to provide any standards as to what is an enemy combatant, and presented no evidence that Hamdi was an enemy or a combatant, a three-judge court of appeals panel ignored these realities and surrendered its judicial authority to the government. The U.S. Court of Appeals for the Fourth Circuit fell prey to fears of losing the war on terror and decided that it was acceptable for the president to be given king-like powers during times of war. The court found that it is "inappropriate and inconsistent" for the judiciary to question the validity of the president's decision-making power as commander-in-chief.

Many of my fellow conservatives have welcomed reposing this kind and amount of power into President Bush's hands. He is a good man, they tell me, big-hearted, clear-headed, modest, honest, and trustworthy. I, too, believe he is. But we are a nation of laws, not men, and no president is president forever. Would my friends agree to have given these king-like powers to President Bush's predecessor, or to one of his successors, especially if she has the same last name as the predecessor?

I think not.

Chief Judge Harvie Wilkinson in voting to reverse Judge Doumar conceded that the Mobbs Declaration had "evidentiary shortcomings," yet he opined that it is acceptable to "trust the judgment of those actually fighting the war that Hamdi was properly seized" even though "there is a value to having the U.S. state under oath its reasons for the detention." It is inconceivable that a court could acknowledge that there are "evidentiary shortcomings," but allow an American to remain locked in a military brig indefinitely. The government cannot successfully prosecute a jaywalker with "evidentiary shortcomings!"

Even with evidentiary shortcomings, we know from various sources that the U.S. military paid bounties to Afghan warlords and Pakistani intelligence services for many of the detainees. Who would trust them? Are there any credible witnesses to Hamdi's alleged behavior? Isn't it more likely than not that Hamdi was merely an adversary of the warlords and intelligence agents who may have sold him to the U.S. military?

The appellate court failed to recognize that Hamdi is entitled to protections under the Constitution. It simply asserted that "the Constitution does not specifically contemplate any role for the courts in the conduct of war."

The Constitution, which specifically denies to the government the power to strip us of our rights, ("No person shall . . . be deprived of life, liberty, or property, without due process of law.") means the same in war as in peace; the Supreme Court told us that in *Milligan*. It is not the conduct of war that is under scrutiny; it is the conduct of the American government threatening one of its citizens.

If the president attempts to destroy these rights, the courts must serve as the final protectors of these rights. Thus, while there may be no specific role for the courts in second guessing battlefield decisions during a war, courts *always* have the duty to ensure that inalienable rights remain inalienable.

In February 2004, the government finally allowed Hamdi's lawyer, Frank Dunham, to meet his client. Dunham noted that, upon entering the interview room, he found "a naval commander" who was there to observe their conversation, and "hovering over [us] was a video camera, its red light brightly lit." Furthermore, the commander prevented Dunham from asking Hamdi about his treatment or interrogations by the military. This clearly violates Hamdi's Sixth Amendment right to the "assistance of counsel for his defense," since "counsel" requires at a minimum the ability to speak in confidence and candor about all aspects of the case without the government and its camera in the room.

Most interestingly, the government, maintaining that the right to counsel is a "matter of discretion" because Hamdi has not been charged with a crime, allowed Hamdi to meet with his lawyer because the Department of Defense had "completed intelligence collection from that combatant." Even though the government admitted that Hamdi possessed no intelligence value whatsoever, it still has no intention of ever charging Hamdi with a crime and bringing him before a court.

The government's pitiful explanation is that it is afraid Hamdi will return to Afghanistan and rejoin the enemy. If the government's fear is justified because Hamdi is truly a war criminal, it should have no difficulty in trying and convicting him of treason. If Hamdi really did not commit any crimes, the government has no power to detain him because of an irrational fear that he *might* join the enemy at some time in the future. The essence of the Constitution's due process guarantee is that the government has no power to lock up an innocent individual just so that the individual is incapable of future criminal behavior.

The cases of Padilla and Hamdi are not "apples and oranges," despite the contention of the U.S. Circuit Court of Appeals for the Fourth Circuit that they are. Judge Wilkinson suggested that Hamdi is less entitled to his constitutional rights because he was captured in Afghanistan rather than Chicago. That distinction is irrelevant, as the rights and privileges of the Constitution are guaranteed to all citizens, wherever they are in the world (". . . at all times and under all circumstances . . .") and no matter how "evil" the government alleges them to be. The president is not the supreme law of the land, the Constitution is.

HAMDI FALLOUT

And the Constitution still lives.

On June 28, 2004, the Supreme Court ruled that the government abused its powers in detaining Hamdi indefinitely and incommunicado and stripping him of all his constitutional rights. By a vote of eight-to-one, the court ordered that Hamdi (and by implication any person the president declares to be an enemy combatant) was entitled to consult freely and privately with counsel from day one, must have charges filed against him, can compel the government to prove those charges, and can challenge the government in court at every turn.

Writing for the court's four-justice plurality, Justice Sandra Day O'Connor admonished the government, ruling that "a state of war is not a blank check for the president when it comes to the rights of the Nation's citizens" because citizens always retain "core rights to challenge meaningfully the Government's case [against them] and to be heard by an impartial adjudicator."

Three judges of vastly different ideologies—liberal (Justice Steven Breyer), moderate (Justice Anthony Kennedy), and conservative (Chief Justice William Rehnquist)—joined Justice O'Connor's opinion.

In a scorching opinion, Justice Antonin Scalia, the Court's most conservative jurist, became the harshest critic of the Bush administration's disregard for constitutionally protected liberties. Justice John Paul Stevens, a liberal member of the Court, joined Scalia. Justice Scalia condemned the government's unprecedented and unconstitutional detention of Hamdi, since "the very core of liberty secured by our Anglo-Saxon system . . . has been freedom from indefinite imprisonment at the will of the Executive."

Expressing the Founding Fathers' "general mistrust of military power permanently at the Executive's disposal," Justice Scalia explained why the Constitution limits the federal government's ability to detain American citizens in wartime: "[T]he 'blessings of liberty' [a]re threatened by 'those military establishments which must gradually poison its very fountain.'"

Two of the court's liberal jurists—Justices David Souter and Ruth Bader Ginsburg—determined that Congress never authorized the federal government to detain indefinitely individuals and deprive them of their constitutional rights. In their opinion, neither the AUMF nor any other Act of Congress provided for such presidential power, even in a time of war. Additionally, they said Hamdi's detention violated the Geneva Conventions.

The court's lone dissenter, Justice Clarence Thomas, agreed with the government's contention that its power is almost unlimited in a time of war.

PREVENTION AND TREASON

The government's continued use of its self-created "enemy combatant" law is proof that power corrupts. As of now, it is begrudgingly complying with the Supreme Court's ruling, but it is resisting at every turn, dragging out the constitutional drama instead of simply doing the right thing.

The circumstances surrounding the detention of Ali Saleh Kahlah al-Marri present a clear example of how the government uses the "enemy combatant" designation as a substitute for evidence.

Al-Marri, a Qatari man who entered the United States in 2001 on a student visa, was arrested in December 2001 as a material witness in the terrorism investigation. Of course, as we know from Judge Scheindlin's experience, the government's decision to name someone a material witness frequently means only that it wants to arrest someone but has no evidence on which to do so. Previously, FBI agents had searched his computer and found bookmarks for identity theft Web sites and twelve hundred credit card numbers, which the agents deemed "a treasure trove of fraud and hacking material."

A grand jury indicted Al-Marri charging him with credit card fraud and making false statements to the FBI. A trial was scheduled to begin in a federal district court on July 22, 2003. The government must have realized the case against Al-Marri was weak, as there was no evidence that Al-Marri used any of the credit card numbers and only accessed identity theft Web sites that were publicly available to anyone surfing the Web. According to Al-Marri's attorney, the government was "unfairly trying to buttress a weak credit card case with unproven allegations about terrorism."

A month before the scheduled trial, the federal government mysteriously dropped the charges against Al-Marri and named him an enemy combatant. He was removed from the Justice Department's custody and delivered into military custody; to the same Navy brig in South Carolina as Padilla and Hamdi, where he is being held indefinitely and incommunicado.

On his client's behalf, Al-Marri's attorney filed an application for *habeas corpus* relief in U.S. District Court in Illinois. The court declined even to consider the rape of Al-Marri's constitutional rights. The court ruled that Al-Marri couldn't bring a *habeas corpus* application in Illinois because the government had transferred him to South Carolina. This interpretation of the law was, as we know, embraced by the Supreme Court in *Padilla*. Now, a lawyer may expect to chase his or her client to and from whatever jails the government wishes. Is that just? Don't the federal courts have jurisdiction over his jailer?

Once again, the government's lawyers—who have sworn a solemn oath to uphold the Constitution—are ignoring the parts of the Constitution they do not like, so as to advance the goals in the war on terror. And once again, courts refuse to step in and become an effective check on the executive branch's self-delegated king-like powers.

Attorney General Ashcroft's rationale for holding Al-Marri incommunicado was, "prevention being our No. 1 objective, we decided we would be best served with him detained as an enemy combatant." The federal government felt that it would be able to obtain more information from Al-Marri if he were placed in military custody since he wasn't cooperating with those prosecuting him. Who would cooperate with one's prosecutors?

Attorney General Ashcroft fails to realize that there is no exception to the Constitution's guaranteed rights when the government's "No. 1 objective" is "prevention." The federal government is not above the rule of law. There are no cases in American history in which our courts have sanctioned punishment before trial as "prevention" against future crimes; and no attorney general—save the present—has ever claimed that power with a straight face. The constitutional and due process rights of Padilla, Hamdi, and al-Marri are inalienable, and neither the government nor the courts may strip them away.

Waging war against the United States by a U.S. citizen is a crime. It is the only crime defined in the Constitution: treason. The administration is perfectly capable of effectively fighting the war on terror within the bounds of the law. If the government has evidence of treason against these three men, why not bring them to trial?

12

DON'T GO
TO GUANTANAMO

After the war in Afghanistan was over, the Defense Department disregarded the constitutional rights of approximately six hundred fifty individuals that the government began bringing to Camp Delta at the U.S. Naval Base on Guantanamo Bay, Cuba, and holding there incommunicado. None of these individuals has been charged with a crime, let alone been found guilty of one. Yet, the government seeks to keep all of these individuals indefinitely locked away, barred from consulting with a lawyer, and without ever appearing before a court.

The U.S. military obtained custody of most of these persons from various sources during late 2001 and early 2002, shortly after the United States entered into hostilities against the Taliban in Afghanistan. For almost three years, and potentially for the rest of their lives, the U.S. military has treated these individuals as subhuman. By maintaining dilapidated conditions and pursuing psychological torture, the U.S. military is violating the human rights protections guaranteed under the Geneva Conventions. Of course, the federal government claims that it isn't bound to abide by international law, because that would also imply that these detainees would be allowed access to legal counsel and a hearing before an impartial tribunal.

At the request of U.S. military authorities, the Afghan Northern Alliance initially rounded up many of these detainees, mostly with the aid of bounty hunters and Afghani warlords. Thousands of detainees were kidnapped, handcuffed, blindfolded, shackled, and placed into airtight containers. These containers were brought to an Afghani prison, where it was determined that at least fifty individuals died from lack of food and water, suffocation, and lack of medical aid. Some were murdered when the U.S. military allegedly directed Afghan prison guards to shoot bullets into the containers, while prisoners were still inside, to create air holes!

When the U.S. military transported the prisoners from Afghanistan to the Navy Base at Guantanamo Bay, the detainees were shackled to the aircraft seats and blindfolded with special blacked-out goggles throughout the twenty-four-hour flight. According to a *Los Angeles Times* report, the federal government now admits it had determined that, before the prisoners were even transferred to Guantanamo Bay, over 10 percent of them neither committed any war crimes nor had any intelligence value! Furthermore, General Michael Dunlavey, the operational commander at Camp Delta, complained to his bosses in the Defense Department that the prison was overcrowded with "Mickey Mouse detainees."

At Camp Delta, the detainees are confined to small wire cages with concrete floors. These "cells" are open to the elements, including rats, snakes, and scorpions that are loose around the base. Jamal al-Harith, a detainee who was never charged with a crime and was eventually released in March 2004, was a victim of brutal psychological torture in an effort to bring about a confession. (A confession to what?) He explained how the U.S. military hired prostitutes to be vice girls, in order to shock and torment the most religiously devout Muslims. These prostitutes danced naked in front of the prisoners, and one even smeared menstrual blood across al-Harith's face in an act of humiliation.

The conditions are so devastating at Guantanamo Bay that there have been at least twenty-eight suicide attempts by eighteen individuals. Shah Muhammad tried four times to hang himself. After his second suicide attempt, he was given tranquilizer tablets so the military could encourage his cooperation with his interrogators. The military even told him, truthfully, that he had committed no crime and was only being held for questioning. But once again, he attempted suicide. Military physicians forcefully administered a powerful injection that left him unable to control his head or mouth or eat properly for weeks. For reasons not articulated publicly, the government thinks it can get away with violating the Constitution and treating individuals as such, even when it *knows* that those individuals are entirely innocent.

HABEAS CORPUS, NO

The government lumped each of these 650 prisoners into the "enemy combatant" category, as it had done with Jose Padilla, Yasir Hamdi, and Ali al-Marri. In early 2002, sixteen of these prisoners filed applications for a writ of *habeas corpus*, seeking to appear before a federal judge to challenge their illegal imprisonment.

Habeas corpus is a right guaranteed to all persons confined against their will. This right—which dates back to the Magna Carta—is guaranteed in the U.S. Constitution and several federal statutes. The Constitution declares that only Congress can suspend *habeas corpus*, and it may do so only in a time of invasion. Congress has *never* suspended that right.

The first of these cases, *Rasul v. Bush*, was filed against the government on February 19, 2002. In that case, four prisoners being held by the U.S. military indefinitely and incommunicado—two from the United Kingdom and two from Australia—challenged their detention. Little detail is known about the precise circumstances of the capture of these four individuals (because the federal government won't give them their day in court!), but they appear to have been transferred to U.S. custody in December 2001. Each detainee asserted that at no time did he voluntarily join any military or terrorist force.

British citizen Shafiq Rasul stated that, in the summer of 2001, he took a hiatus from his computer engineering studies in order to travel throughout Pakistan. He was living at his aunt's home in Lahore, Pakistan, so that he could visit relatives and explore his culture. Rasul alleged that, as he left his aunt's home one day, forces that were fighting *against* the United States captured and kidnapped him.

Asif Iqbal, another Briton, alleged that he traveled to Pakistan in September 2001 to get married to a woman living in his father's Pakistani village. He briefly left the village and was captured, he says, by other forces fighting *in opposition* to the American military.

Even less is known about the capture of the two Australians. David Hicks was living in Afghanistan in late 2001 when he was seized by the Northern Alliance, a group of warlords loosely affiliated with American forces. He alleged that he was providing humanitarian assistance to the Afghani people. The other Australian, Mamdouh Habib, says he was in Pakistan to find a school for his two children. He was most likely arrested by Pakistani officials at the Pakistan-Afghanistan border in October 2001, and was secretly brought to Egypt before he was handed over to U.S. authorities.

A second case against the government was filed on May 1, 2002. In *Al Odah v. United States,* twelve Kuwaiti nationals being held indefinitely and incommunicado at Camp Delta asked a federal court in Washington, D.C., to grant them access to their attorneys and to have access to "the courts or some other impartial tribunal." These detainees didn't even demand to be released from confinement. They simply sought to exercise their *habeas corpus* rights as guaranteed to them by the Constitution.

These twelve individuals were in Afghanistan and Pakistan in late 2001. Pursuant to a Kuwaiti national policy of paying the salaries of government employees who go abroad to volunteer for charitable purposes, these individuals were in those countries to provide humanitarian aid. Their petition stated that none of them had ever been a combatant or belligerent against the U.S., nor a supporter of the Taliban or any other terrorist organization. They alleged that they were seized, against their will, not by the U.S. military, but by villagers seeking bounties or other promised financial rewards.

A federal district court judge in Washington, D.C., denied the *habeas corpus* relief for all sixteen of these detainees.

Judge Colleen Kollar-Kotelly ruled that no United States court has jurisdiction to hear the cases. The federal government convinced the judge to ignore over a hundred years of judicial precedent in order to find that the U.S. Navy base at Guantanamo Bay, Cuba, is "outside the sovereign territory of the United States." This ruling completely ignores the 1903 lease agreement between the U.S. and Cuba, which provides that the U.S. exercises "complete jurisdiction and control over and within [the Guantanamo Bay Naval Base]."

Despite this clear statement indicating that a U.S. district court would have jurisdiction over the detainees, the government relied on an irrelevant phrase in the lease that affirmed Cuba's retention of the "ultimate sovereignty" over Guantanamo Bay, and convinced the court that the sovereign power over the U.S. military and others at Guantanamo Bay belongs to *Fidel Castro*. Tell that to the commanding American naval officer!

The U.S. Court of Appeals for the District of Columbia Circuit affirmed the district judge's absurd ruling. Splitting jurisprudential hairs, the court held that "territorial jurisdiction" is not the same thing as "sovereignty." If the U.S. has "territorial jurisdiction" over the Naval Base, how can a federal court not have jurisdiction over persons detained there? The court continued its absurd line of reasoning by ruling that courts have noted a distinction between "friendly aliens" and "enemy aliens."

This erroneous reasoning was derived from the 1950 U.S. Supreme Court case of *Johnson v. Eisentrager*. In that case, twenty-one German nationals sought to provide assistance to the Japanese military, in the summer of 1945, between the German and Japanese surrenders. They were captured by U.S. forces in China, tried and convicted of war crimes by an American military commission in China, and were imprisoned in Landsberg Prison in occupied Germany. The Court denied these "enemy aliens" the ability to apply to U.S. courts for *habeas corpus* review, because they had never been to the U.S. and were captured, tried, and imprisoned outside of the U.S.

Without any basis for doing so, the Court of Appeals reviewing Judge Kollar-Kotelly's ruling concluded that the sixteen detainees being held at Guantanamo Bay were also "enemy aliens outside the U.S." The German nationals in *Eisentrager* were convicted war criminals; when did any U.S. court or military tribunal ever determine that these sixteen detainees in Cuba were the "enemy"? Never. The court simply dwelled on an irrelevant throwaway term in order to disregard the constitutional rights of these individuals.

A separate action, *Coalition of Clergy v. Bush*, was filed on January 20, 2002, in federal district court in Los Angeles, California. A group of law and journalism professors, rabbis, ministers, and a former U.S. attorney general requested *habeas corpus* relief on behalf of *all* of the detainees being held at Guantanamo Bay. The court dismissed the application on a procedural point, ruling that the applicants had no standing—no right to commence a lawsuit—because none had a "significant relationship with the detainees." Equating the group of plaintiffs to "uninvited meddlers," the court stated there was "[no] evidence that they are welcome."

The U.S. government refused to allow the detainees to consult with anyone—lawyers, family members, clergy, members of the group—so there can't possibly be any evidence that anyone is not "welcome" to act on behalf of the detainees. Effectively, the government and the courts created a blockade whereby neither the detainees themselves nor individuals acting on their behalf could argue before a court that anyone's constitutional rights were being violated.

Subsequently, the group found a detainee—Belaid Gherebi—whose brother had standing to petition the court for *habeas corpus* relief on his behalf. However, Judge Howard Matz—the same judge who came up with the "not welcome" ruling—again dismissed the action, finding another means of circumventing the Constitution in order to allow the government to violate the Camp Delta detainees' due process protections.

The judge mimicked the erroneous rationale of the Court of Appeals for the D.C. Circuit in the *Rasul* and *Al Odah* cases, even though the D.C. Circuit's rulings are not binding on California district courts. Relying on the arbitrary distinction between "complete jurisdiction and control" and "sovereign territory," Judge Matz held that no federal court in the U.S. would be equipped to address Gherebi's constitutional rights. According to Judge Matz, the Camp Delta detainees must hope for "Presidential intervention" because they have no means of enforcing their constitutional rights.

The principal function of the judicial branch is to preserve the rights guaranteed by the Constitution. Judge Matz even noted that for "more than fifteen months . . . not one Guantanamo detainee has been given the opportunity to consult an attorney, has had formal charges filed against him or has been able to contest the basis for his detention. . . . *This lengthy delay is not consistent with some of the most basic values our legal system has long embodied*" (my emphasis). If he holds these values, why didn't Judge Matz act to defend the Constitution rather than sit back and let the government have unlimited wartime powers?

HABEAS CORPUS, YES!

In a victory for constitutional liberties, the Court of Appeals for the Ninth Circuit reversed Judge Matz's ruling. In *Gherebi v. Bush*, the Ninth Circuit, unlike the D.C. Circuit, refused to parrot the government's flawed reliance on the 1903 lease between the U.S. and Cuba.

The court ruled that federal courts do have jurisdiction to address the detainees' *habeas corpus* applications, since "even in times of national emergency . . . it is the obligation of the Judicial Branch to ensure the preservation of our constitutional values and to prevent the Executive Branch from running roughshod over the rights of citizens and aliens alike." Furthermore, the court refused to allow the government to rely on "counter-intuitive and undemocratic" flawed legal arguments to give itself "unchecked authority to imprison indefinitely any persons . . . on territory under the sole jurisdiction and control of the United States, without . . . recourse . . . to any judicial forum, or even access to counsel."

The Court of Appeals for the Ninth Circuit went even further and noted numerous examples of the federal government itself acknowledging that Guantanamo Bay was "within the United States." Most notably, the court cited a 1982 memorandum written by then Assistant Attorney General Theodore Olson. In that memorandum, Olson concluded that Guantanamo Bay falls within "exclusive United States' jurisdiction . . . because of the lease terms which grant the United States 'complete jurisdiction and control over' that property." *Exclusive* jurisdiction!

Mr. Olson—at the time these cases were argued Solicitor General Olson, the government's chief litigator before the U.S. Supreme Court—maintained on behalf of the government *in this case* that Guantanamo Bay was "outside the United States." Can the government make up its mind? The only thing that changed in the last twenty-two years with respect to United States control over Guantanamo Bay is that the government now seeks to ignore the Constitution when it comes to the *habeas corpus* rights of those being detained there.

The U.S. Supreme Court reviewed the split between the Ninth and D.C. Circuits on the issue of whether Camp Delta at Guantanamo Bay is "within the U.S." or "outside the U.S." On June 28, 2004, the Supreme Court ruled six to three that federal courts have jurisdiction to review the Camp Delta detainees' *habeas corpus* applications.

Justice John Paul Stevens, writing for the Court, went so far as to conclude that it wouldn't even matter whether a federal court had jurisdiction *over the prisoners.* He concluded that, pursuant to a 1973 Supreme Court decision (*Braden v. 30th Judicial Circuit Court of Kentucky*) interpreting the federal *habeas corpus* statute, jurisdiction is based on whether the federal court has jurisdiction *over the prisoners' custodian.* Since the Camp Delta prison custodian received and accepted the complaints filed against him, a federal court is authorized to review the detainees' claims that the custodian is illegally imprisoning them. Besides, the ultimate custodian is the secretary of defense, over whom federal courts no doubt have jurisdiction.

The Court also rejected the government's argument that Guantanamo Bay was outside the United States' territorial sovereignty. During oral arguments, Solicitor General Olson conceded that federal courts would have jurisdiction to review an application for *habeas corpus* brought by an American citizen detained at Camp Delta. Accordingly, the court determined that this established that Camp Delta is within the United States. And since the *habeas corpus* statute "draws no distinction between Americans and aliens held in federal custody," the court ruled that "aliens held at the base, no less than American citizens, are entitled to invoke the federal courts' authority." Thus, the court pointedly determined that the Constitution protects all *persons*—citizens and non-citizens—from the U.S. government's attempt to deprive them of their guaranteed rights.

The Supreme Court also dismissed the government's incessant reliance on the *Eisentrager* court's finding that the German nationals held at the Landsberg Prison could not have access to U.S. courts. The Court determined that the Guantanamo Bay detainees were "differently situated" than the German prisoners. Unlike the German prisoners, the detainees "are not nationals of countries at war with the United States, and they deny that they have engaged in or plotted acts of aggression against the United States; they have never been afforded access to any tribunal, much less charged with and convicted of any wrongdoing; and for more than two years they have been imprisoned in a territory over which the United States [has] exercised exclusive jurisdiction and control." Therefore, the court held, not only does the *habeas corpus* guarantee provide the Camp Delta detainees with access to federal courts, but the Constitution's due process requirement also mandates that the detainees are entitled to their day in court.

GUILTY? WHO KNOWS?

At the time of the Supreme Court's ruling, 594 detainees remained in U.S. military custody at Camp Delta. The government released approximately 134 of the detainees due to diplomatic and political pressure. British Prime Minister Tony Blair, under pressure from his own citizenry, made a secret plea to President Bush seeking the release of the detained Britons. Shortly thereafter, the U.S. military released five Britons, in order to maintain strong relations with its closest ally.

These individuals could very well be guilty of war crimes, but there is no way to know because the government refused to grant them hearings. Justice is not served when the government imprisons innocent people because it can get away with it and possibly exonerates guilty people because it wishes to maintain political relationships.

Some of these 594 detainees may have committed war crimes against the United States, while others may be innocent victims of rogue bounty hunters. Hamed Abderrahman Ahmad, an accused Al Qaeda member who was detained at Camp Delta from late 2001 to February 2004, was turned over to Spain only at the request of his native government. And on July 14, 2004, Ahmad posted bail in the amount of $3,707 and finally saw freedom. Clearly, the U.S. had detained an innocent individual; courts set extraordinarily low bail amounts for petty criminals, not known terrorists. How many other Camp Delta detainees are similarly innocent?

Had the Supreme Court not stepped in and prevented the government from ignoring the Constitution, we might never have been able to separate the innocent from the guilty.

In August 2004, in an effort to avoid having to present evidence at any public *habeas corpus* hearings and in a begrudging response to the Supreme Court, the U.S. military began holding in secret what it called Combat Status Review Tribunals (CSRTs) in order to ascertain the true enemy status—two and a half years after capture—of the remaining detainees. At these CSRTs, the government was represented by counsel, the detainees by non-lawyer advisers. On September 8, 2004, Navy Secretary Gordon England announced that the first of the detainees to have his status reviewed was determined not to be an enemy combatant as defined by the government, and soon would be returned to his home country. Can anyone seriously suggest that this result would have come about without the ruling of the Supreme Court?

CHANGING THE RULES

As if the Supreme Court's ruling as to the legal status of Guantanamo Bay wasn't enough of a blow to the government, a classified Defense Department memorandum, leaked to the media three weeks before the court's ruling addressing that same issue, illustrates in a biting way the hypocrisy and duplicity of the federal government.

In the detainee cases before the Supreme Court, the government's excuse for ignoring the Constitution was that the Navy Base on Guantanamo Bay was not within the United States. However, in a March 2003 memorandum advising the president on how to avoid a federal law prohibiting the U.S. military from torturing prisoners held at Guantanamo Bay, the Pentagon advised the president that Guantanamo Bay *is* "within the United States." The Pentagon explained to the president that the federal statute that criminalizes torture does not apply to the conduct of the U.S. military within the United States. The statute requires that the torture occur "outside the United States," for a successful prosecution of U.S. military personnel.

In the memorandum, Defense Department lawyers argued that Guantanamo Bay is "included within the definition of the special maritime and territorial jurisdiction of the United States, and accordingly, is within the United States." Based on its contention that Guantanamo Bay was *not* "outside the United States," the Defense Department advised the president that U.S. military personnel were immunized from prosecution for torture committed at Guantanamo Bay under this statute.

The memorandum further expounds upon the government's position that Guantanamo Bay is within the United States. Several examples of the government's recognition of federal courts having jurisdiction over Guantanamo Bay are given; there are numerous instances of the government using federal district courts on the U.S. mainland to prosecute civilian dependants and employees living on the Navy Base. Furthermore, the memo states that support for the contention that the U.S. possesses territorial jurisdiction over Guantanamo Bay is found in the "clear intention of Congress as reflected in [the PATRIOT Act]."

A classified Department of Justice memorandum advising the president on how to avoid the federal statute prohibiting torture likewise implies that Guantanamo Bay is within the United States. This memo, dated August 1, 2002, and authored by then Assistant Attorney General Jay Bybee (now Judge Bybee of the U.S. Court of Appeals for the Ninth Circuit), appears to dodge the issue of Guantanamo Bay's legal status. However, a footnote all but expresses the contention that Guantanamo Bay falls into the definition of "within the United States."

Just as the Pentagon memorandum stated, the Justice Department memorandum expresses the proposition that the special maritime and territorial jurisdiction of the U.S. is considered "within the United States." While the island isn't directly referenced, it is unequivocally clear that Guantanamo Bay, Cuba, falls into that classification.

The government's two positions on the legal status of Guantanamo Bay represent bipolar extremes. When the government wants to avoid a torture statute that applies outside the United States, it argues that Guantanamo Bay is within the U.S. But when Camp Delta detainees seek access to federal courts to challenge their illegal confinement, Guantanamo Bay suddenly becomes "outside the United States."

Is Congress rewriting the law every few weeks when the government seeks a new way to achieve its goals in the war on terror? No. The government is simply stretching and twisting federal law and the Constitution in whatever way it sees fit for whatever contemporary need it may have.

The government can't have it both ways: it must argue either that Guantanamo Bay is under the jurisdiction of federal courts, or that it is not. These two positions cannot be reconciled by anything short of perverse legal reasoning. This duplicity is expressly barred by the doctrine of *judicial estoppel,* which prevents any litigant in any American court from arguing two different ways as to the same point of law.

Not only can the government not argue two ways, but it cannot have the law both ways. The president can't send government lawyers to the Supreme Court to argue that the Constitution and federal law *do not* apply at Guantanamo Bay, while at the same time receiving advice from the lawyers that federal law *does* indeed apply at Guantanamo Bay.

The federal government's duplicity and hypocrisy with respect to whether the Constitution applies at Guantanamo Bay arose once again when the U.S. military filed charges against one of its own servicemen stationed at Camp Delta.

On January 27, 2004, Senior Airman Ahman al-Halabi was arrested and charged with espionage and aiding the enemy. The Defense Department alleged that al-Halabi made illegal contact with his native Syria, attempting to deliver classified information to the Embassy of Syria about the movement of the detainees being held at Camp Delta. By charging al-Halabi with committing a federal crime at Guantanamo Bay, the federal government is undoubtedly conceding that federal laws apply there and thus that the Constitution applies as well. This is diametrically opposite to the argument the government made to the U.S. Supreme Court in the detainee cases!

Isn't it ironic that the government upholds the Constitution as to Al-Halabi—an Air Force translator who was employed by the U.S. military to communicate with the Camp Delta detainees—but denies those same detainees their constitutional protections? The Supreme Court has ruled countless times that the concept of the Constitution as a cafeteria—take the powers you want, Attorney General John Ashcroft; leave the rights you don't want—has no place in our jurisprudence.

PART 4

PROSPECTS FOR LIBERTY

13

WHAT CAN WE DO?

It is clear that the government has a free hand when it comes to prose-cuting people for both genuine and government-created crimes, while disregarding the Constitution in the process. But let us not lose sight of the fact that we are still a free society, and, notwithstanding a huge, entrenched bureaucracy, those who set policy in the executive and legislative branches are still popularly elected.

Ultimately, the fate of American liberty is in the hands of American voters. Though we are less free with every tick of the clock, most of us still believe that the government is supposed to serve the people—fairly, not selectively.

There are some surprisingly direct ways to address the excesses described in this book.

APPLY THE LAW TO EVERYONE

First, Congress and the state legislatures should enact legislation simply requiring that the police and all law enforcement personnel, and everyone who works for or is an agent of the government, be governed by, subject to, and required to comply with all the laws.

This, of course, would render useless arguments like "the bribery statute doesn't apply to the government." This would also prevent police officers from walking through Washington Square Park and attempting to sell drugs in the presence of children. This would eliminate virtually all entrapment, and it would enhance respect for the law. How many times have you seen a police officer turn on a siren to go through a red light or park in front of a fire hydrant or drive the wrong way down a one-way street for no apparent reason (perhaps, to invoke a cynical stereotype, just to get donuts and coffee)?

Theoretically, if the police are required to obey the same laws as the rest of us, our respect for them and for the laws they enforce would dramatically increase, and their jobs would become easier. This would also mean that no person could be prosecuted for any crime if, during the lead up to the prosecution, the police committed a crime. In short, it would be against the law to break the law. It may seem silly to suggest that the government adopt a law stating that the government must follow the law, but the many instances of government law-breaking and abuse outlined in this book demonstrate that such a law enforcing the law is necessary.

SUE THE BASTARDS

Congress and the state legislatures should also make it easier to sue the federal and state governments for monetary damages when they violate our constitutional liberties.

The federal government and many states have rendered themselves immune (called "sovereign immunity") from such lawsuits if the lawsuit attacks the exercise of discretion by government employees. This is nonsense. You can sue your neighbor for negligence if his car runs over your garden or your dog. You can sue a corporation if it pollutes the air you breathe. You can sue your physician if he leaves a scalpel in your belly.

You should be able to sue the local police, state police, and the FBI under the same legal theories if they torment you, if they prevent you from speaking freely, if they bribe witnesses to testify against you, if they steal your property, or if they break the law in order to convict you.

Along with removing sovereign immunity, I would also remove personal immunity on the part of individuals who work for the government when they commit crimes. Let me explain what I mean.

If a corporation harms you by selling you a defective product, you may sue the individuals who work for the corporation who actually caused the defect, as well as the corporation itself. The individuals are usually indemnified, that is, their legal bills are paid and any settlements or judgments against them are paid by the corporation which employs them. If they have committed a crime during the course of their employment which led to the defect, their employer cannot indemnify them, and they are personally exposed to your lawsuit. The same should be the case for government employees and agents. If a government employee commits a crime in the course of his work, he should lose all immunity and be exposed personally to litigation by the victim of the crime. This would be a strong and cost-effective way to compel the government, its employees, and agents to obey the same laws they are sworn to enforce.

In some states and in the federal system, if a litigant files a frivolous pleading with the court or makes an indefensible argument to the court, the litigant must pay the legal fees of his adversary for resisting the pleading or the argument. This rule should be applied as well to the federal and state governments in civil and in criminal cases. If a defendant is ultimately exonerated in a criminal case, and the government broke the law to prosecute him, the government should pay his legal bills.

DEFEND THE CONSTITUTION

My political friends have often attacked the concept of "judicial activism." By this they mean they strongly condemn a judge's substitution of his or her judgments for that of the legislature or the executive. Let's be brutally honest about this: The only judicial activism we condemn is that with which we disagree. One man's judicial activism is another man's heroic defense of the Constitution. When judicial activism merely enforces the Constitution, it is a very good concept.

If, for example, a state legislature were to enact a statute authorizing the enslavement of household domestic help, a judge would surely strike the statute down as being in violation of the Thirteenth Amendment. Would anyone call that judicial activism?

If Congress were to enact a statute making it a criminal offense to criticize the Congress, and a judge were to invalidate the statute as being in violation of the First Amendment, would anyone call that judicial activism?

The answers to these questions are clear because the violations of the Constitution are clear. Judges are attacked for being judicial activists only by those who disagree with the judges' decisions. In my two hypotheticals there would be some people who would attack the acts of these judges as judicial activism: those who wanted to possess slaves and incumbent members of Congress.

On the other side of judicial activism is judicial tyranny. If, for example, a teachers' union thinks a city should budget more money for its teachers' salaries, and the mayor says no, and the union sues and gets a judge to agree, and the judge orders the city to pay higher salaries, that judicial act is tyrannical. Why? It is within the institutional function of the judiciary to say what the Constitution means; it is not within the judicial function—its competence—to raise taxes, fix salaries, or set a budget. Those functions are expressly given by law to the other two branches of government. Judges should only invalidate the acts of Congress or the president in cases of clear contradiction of the Constitution and when natural rights have been impaired.

Please do not forget that the American system of government is not a democracy, it is a republic; and it has features that are distinctly anti-democratic. To paraphrase Professor Laurence Tribe of Harvard Law School, the whole reason we have an independent, life-tenured federal judiciary is to put brakes on democracy, to prevent the tyranny of the majority. Without a judiciary checking the behavior of Congress and the president—making certain they conform to the Constitution—nothing could prevent the majority from taking property or freedom from those it despised.

HOLDING CHAOS AT BAY

The ultimate lesson of this book is that for the government, crime pays. It makes prosecution easier and virtually guarantees success.

When a person or corporation breaks the law, they are prosecuted and, if convicted, they are punished. Theoretically, the punishment makes society whole, as best we can do in a free society. We don't any longer believe in an eye for an eye or a tooth for a tooth. We somehow accept the idea that a robber who steals ten thousand dollars from a bank and, after conviction, is forced to return it and serve ten years in jail, has wiped his slate clean; and that a polluter who has harmed the waters or the air, but has been made to pay the cost of cleaning up the pollution and serve jail time, has also wiped the slate clean.

But when the government commits a crime, and the offending government actors are not prosecuted, it becomes a *precedent*; no slate is wiped clean.

Worse, the precedent becomes a basis for the same government and other governments to do likewise in the future. The precedent breeds disrespect and frustration. The precedent tramples human liberties, and it makes those who run the government, however brief their tenure, close to tyrants. The precedent is contagious because unpunished crime is contagious; it breeds contempt for law and invites some to become a law unto themselves.

If the Constitution is enforced selectively, according to the contemporary wants and needs of the government, we will continue to see public trials in Detroit and secret trials in Newark; free speech suppressed on inexplicable whims; police targeting the weak and killing the innocent;

government lying to its citizens, stealing their property, tricking them into criminal acts, bribing its witnesses against them, making a mockery of legal reasoning, and breaking the laws in order to enforce them. A government that commits crime is not your friend.

This is not the type of government we, the people, have authorized to exist, and it is not the type of government that we should tolerate. We can do better. If government crimes are not checked, our Constitution will be meaningless, and our attempts to understand and enforce and rely on it will be chaotic.

APPENDIX

INTRODUCTION TO
THE U.S. CONSTITUTION

The Constitution of the United States is the most examined and debated document in our country's history. It was written as a classic American compromise after months of debate at the Constitutional Convention in Philadelphia, which met during the summer of 1787. Essentially, the document constructs, establishes, and imposes limitations on the federal government by which each of the states gave some of their independent sovereign power away and created a new central government.

THE GREAT COMPROMISE

The Constitution was not the first effort by the states to create a central government. The first effort was the Articles of Confederation. Basically it created an umbrella government, subject to the wishes of the various states, any one of which could disregard a law that the central government enacted. Because of fears that Great Britain, the country from which our colonies broke away, would some day attempt to take back the states—a fear which, of course, came true in 1812—many political leaders felt the Articles of Confederation did not provide the type of central government strong enough to unite the former colonies into one sovereign capable of dealing with all foreign governments with one voice, and strong enough to protect its people.

The Constitution is unique because it indisputably establishes the primacy of the individual over the state. It guarantees liberties and guarantees that the central government will not impair them. Basically, the Constitution is the result of a compromise between Federalists personified by Alexander Hamilton, who wanted a very strong central government, and Anti-Federalists personified by Thomas Jefferson, who wanted strict limitations on the new government's powers and guarantees of liberty. Thus, out of that conflict of ideas, the federal government was born.

THE PRESIDENCY

The Constitution provides for a strong chief executive—not a king—but an executive who is not subject to either of the two branches. What do I mean by this? In the modern European system, the head of the government is the prime minister. The prime minister is also the head of the political party that dominates the legislative branch. The prime minister of most modern European countries is not elected in a popular vote. His parties' representatives are elected to parliament and, if they have a majority in parliament, they choose him as the leader of their party to become the leader of the government. The prime minister's name does not appear on a national ballot as a candidate for that office.

Here in the U.S., of course, the president, though voted for popularly, actually is chosen by electors from the states where the voters chose him. The people vote in each state directly for electors, and the electors promise they will cast their state's electoral votes for the winner of that state's popular vote. Usually the person who wins the national popular vote becomes president; but as the 2000 election exemplified, that is not always the case.

Nevertheless, the Constitution gives us a strong chief executive, not one whose powers derive from the legislature, but one whose powers derive from the Constitution. If a British prime minister loses a vote of confidence, that is, if Parliament rejects one of his proposals, he can be swept from office and forced to stand for re-election; not so with the American president. Not only may he lose a vote in the Congress and still keep his job, but he doesn't even have to be in the same party as that which dominates Congress, and frequently that has been the case.

THE LEGISLATURE

The Congress was created by the Constitution to represent the states and the people. Originally, senators were not popularly elected, but rather elected by state legislatures for six-year terms. Thus, the senators didn't represent the people in a state, they represented the state itself, its government, its sovereignty, in the United States Senate. In 1913, the Constitution was amended to provide for direct popular election of senators.

Members of the House of Representatives have always been popularly elected. The House has always been considered "the peoples' house," and its representatives seek re-election every two years.

Thus, in the two popular branches of government, we see a classic American compromise. In the Senate are representatives of the sovereign states. In the House of Representatives are representatives of the people. In the presidency is a person who must have broad popular support but could actually be elected without it.

THE JUDICIARY

The most peculiar branch, and the least understood, is the judiciary. The judicial branch of the government consists of life-tenured judges appointed by the president and confirmed by the Senate. These judges, of course, never have to seek election and can only be removed from office upon impeachment, after conviction of a felony.

The purpose of the judicial branch, as created by the Constitution, was to hear trials and apply federal laws to the unique cases before them. In the very famous case of *Marbury v. Madison*, however, in 1803, the

Supreme Court decided that its purpose would be grander than that. The Court claimed for itself the power to invalidate acts of the Congress which were inconsistent with the Constitution. At the time, such power was considered a radical notion.

William Marbury had been appointed as a federal magistrate by outgoing President John Adams, a Federalist. His appointment was confirmed by the Senate, but the secretary of state in the Adams administration neglected to give Marbury his formal commission. After Thomas Jefferson, an Anti-Federalist, became president, his secretary of state, James Madison, refused to deliver Marbury his commission. So Marbury sued Madison in the Supreme Court seeking an order to compel Madison to deliver the commission to Marbury. The Supreme Court rejected Marbury's claim, not because he was not entitled to it (he was), but because the Congressional statute under which he sued, which gave the Supreme Court original jurisdiction over this type of lawsuit, was unconstitutional. This was so, the Court ruled, because the Constitution dictates the areas over which the Supreme Court has original jurisdiction, and the Congress cannot alter that. The party that immediately benefited by the outcome of *Marbury v. Madison* was the Anti-Federalists, who were in power at the time, and the result—that Mr. Marbury did not become a magistrate— was then popular. But of course, this power would dog presidents and congresses even up to the present day.

The power is called "judicial review," and it is now universally accepted that not only the Supreme Court, but all federal judges, can review and void acts of Congress or acts of the president which the federal judge is able to demonstrate are inconsistent with the Constitution. For example, if the president were to declare that he did not need to seek reelection and he was entitled to retain his job for life, and a lawsuit were filed challenging that declaration, it would be easy for a federal judge to invalidate the declaration because it is inconsistent with the Constitution which sets the president's term at four years. If Congress were to enact a law that made it unlawful to criticize members of the Congress, it would be easy for a federal judge to invalidate that law as inconsistent with the First Amendment to the Constitution, which guarantees freedom of speech.

I have addressed judicial review at length in this book. It is indeed controversial, but now nearly universally accepted. Sometimes we call the exercise of judicial review judicial activism when we disagree with what the court does; sometimes we call it judicial heroism when we agree with the judicial outcome.

THE BILL OF RIGHTS

The amendments to the Constitution are divided into two categories. The first ten of them are known as the Bill of Rights.

The Bill of Rights was promised to Thomas Jefferson and the Anti-Federalists as a condition for their support for the Constitution. The great fear of the Anti-Federalists—those who if around today would fear Big Government—was that the central government would take personal liberty away from individuals and power away from the states. When the authors of the Constitution guaranteed the Anti-Federalists that the document would contain a Bill of Rights which would spell out the rights and liberties that the Constitution would guarantee, and would retain powers for the states, it was an easier sell in those states concerned about personal freedom and limited government.

When we use the term the Bill of Rights, we are referring only to the first ten amendments to the Constitution. If you read those ten amendments, you will see that they consist of guaranteeing specific individual rights that the federal government cannot take away, and powers that the states will always keep.

After we fought the Civil War, and added the Thirteenth, Fourteenth, and Fifteenth Amendments, the courts began interpreting those, especially the Fourteenth, as meaning that not only can the federal government not interfere with liberties guaranteed in the Bill of Rights, but also, none of the state governments can interfere with them either.

STATE SOVEREIGNTY

The starting point of the Constitution is that the thirteen states which formed the federal government were sovereign and independent states free to go their own way. There was a Continental Congress, of course, in 1776. It had little or no power other than to direct then General George Washington as he waged war against the British. The real political power that existed in 1776 was in the governorship and the legislature of each of the thirteen states.

When those political leaders of those thirteen states agreed that the Articles of Confederation were too weak to allow the country to be perceived as a sovereign unit by foreign countries, each of the states gave away some of their power to form the new central government.

Even though the Constitution begins with "We the people," it was really "We the States" that formed the Constitution. The Constitution itself indicates that it would not come into existence until two thirds of the thirteen states agreed to accept it. So when one thinks of the federal government of the United States of America, one should think of a government with limitations imposed on it by the Constitution and with powers given to it by the various states. This, of course, presumes, and historically this is the case, that the thirteen original states preceded the existence of the federal government and actually, literally gave away some of their powers so as to form a central government. As an example, before 1789, many states issued their own currency and had their own armies. This obviously is something they cannot do under the Constitution because they gave those powers away to the central, federal government.

SEPARATION OF POWERS

The Constitution itself divides power, as we saw earlier, among a president who enforces the laws, a Congress which writes the laws, and a judiciary which interprets the laws. It also, of course, limits the powers of the three branches of government so that they deal with problems that are truly federal in nature. Unfortunately, these limitations have rarely been honored, and throughout the many years of our existence, fanatics and busybodies, do-gooders and collectivists in the congresses have found infamous and duplicitous ways, and power-hungry judges in the courts have bent over backward to allow congresses and presidents, to exercise power never contemplated by the Constitution.

Article 1, section 8 specifically lists only eighteen areas of human behavior over which Congress may legislate, and thus the president may enforce, and the courts may interpret. Those areas involve coining money, regulating interstate and foreign commerce, establishing rules of naturalization, establishing post offices and courts, and supporting an army and navy. The power to regulate all other areas of human behavior that the Natural Law allows governments to regulate was retained by the States. Despite the strict enumeration of congressional powers, the Congress has exercised powers never granted, enumerated, or delegated to it and has regulated, with the courts' approval, everything from automobile speed limits to the amount of sugar in ketchup, from the size of toilet bowls to the wages of janitors, from the fat content of cheese to the number of lobsters you can catch and the amount of wheat you can grow, from the number of pain killers your physician can prescribe to the amount of your income you can keep.

Jefferson and Madison would not be happy with what's become of it, but here is the Constitution, with the Bill of Rights and the other amendments, in all its simple glory. While I've largely left alone the style elements peculiar to when the Constitution was written, I have updated the spellings of a few words for easier readability.

THE CONSTITUTION OF THE UNITED STATES

We the People of the United States, in Order to form a more perfect Union, establish Justice, insure domestic Tranquility, provide for the common defense, promote the general Welfare, and secure the Blessings of Liberty to ourselves and our Posterity, do ordain and establish this Constitution for the United States of America.

ARTICLE 1

Section 1. All legislative Powers herein granted shall be vested in a Congress of the United States, which shall consist of a Senate and House of Representatives.

Section 2. The House of Representatives shall be composed of Members chosen every second Year by the People of the several States, and the Electors in each State shall have the Qualifications requisite for Electors of the most numerous Branch of the State Legislature.

No Person shall be a Representative who shall not have attained to the Age of twenty five Years, and been seven Years a Citizen of the United States, and who shall not, when elected, be an Inhabitant of that State in which he shall be chosen.

Representatives and direct Taxes shall be apportioned among the several States which may be included within this Union, according to their respective Numbers, which shall be determined by adding to the whole Number of free Persons, including those bound to Service for a Term of Years, and excluding Indians not taxed, three fifths of all other Persons.[1] The actual Enumeration shall be made within three Years after the first Meeting of the Congress of the United States, and within every subsequent Term of ten Years, in such Manner as they shall by Law direct. The Number of Representatives shall not exceed one for every thirty Thousand, but each State shall have at Least one Representative; and until such enumeration shall be made, the State of New Hampshire shall be entitled to choose three, Massachusetts eight, Rhode-Island and Providence Plantations one, Connecticut five, New-York six, New Jersey four, Pennsylvania eight, Delaware one, Maryland six, Virginia ten, North Carolina five, South Carolina five, and Georgia three.

When vacancies happen in the Representation from any State,

the Executive Authority thereof shall issue Writs of Election to fill such Vacancies.

The House of Representatives shall choose their Speaker and other Officers; and shall have the sole Power of Impeachment.

Section 3. The Senate of the United States shall be composed of two Senators from each State, chosen by the Legislature[2] thereof for six Years; and each Senator shall have one Vote.

Immediately after they shall be assembled in Consequence of the first Election, they shall be divided as equally as may be into three Classes. The Seats of the Senators of the first Class shall be vacated at the Expiration of the second Year, of the second Class at the Expiration of the fourth Year, and of the third Class at the Expiration of the sixth Year, so that one third may be chosen every second Year; and if Vacancies happen by Resignation, or otherwise, during the Recess of the Legislature of any State, the Executive thereof may make temporary Appointments until the next Meeting of the Legislature, which shall then fill such Vacancies.[3]

No Person shall be a Senator who shall not have attained to the Age of thirty Years, and been nine Years a Citizen of the United States, and who shall not, when elected, be an Inhabitant of that State for which he shall be chosen.

The Vice President of the United States shall be President of the Senate, but shall have no Vote, unless they be equally divided.

The Senate shall choose their other Officers, and also a President pro tempore, in the Absence of the Vice President, or when he shall exercise the Office of President of the United States.

The Senate shall have the sole Power to try all Impeachments. When sitting for that Purpose, they shall be on Oath or Affirmation. When the President of the United States is tried, the Chief Justice shall preside: And no Person shall be convicted without the Concurrence of two thirds of the Members present.

Judgment in Cases of Impeachment shall not extend further than to removal from Office, and disqualification to hold and enjoy any Office of honor, Trust or Profit under the United States: but the Party convicted shall nevertheless be liable and subject to Indictment, Trial, Judgment and Punishment, according to Law.

Section 4. The Times, Places and Manner of holding Elections for Senators and Representatives, shall be prescribed in each State by the Legislature thereof; but the Congress may at any time by Law make or alter such Regulations, except as to the Places of choosing Senators.

The Congress shall assemble at least once in every Year, and such Meeting shall be on the first Monday in December,[4] unless they shall by Law appoint a different Day.

Section 5. Each House shall be the Judge of the Elections, Returns and Qualifications of its own Members, and a Majority of each shall constitute a Quorum to do Business; but a smaller Number may adjourn from day to day, and may be authorized to compel the Attendance of absent Members, in such Manner, and under such Penalties as each House may provide.

Each House may determine the Rules of its Proceedings, punish its Members for disorderly Behavior, and, with the Concurrence of two thirds, expel a Member.

Each House shall keep a Journal of its Proceedings, and from time to time publish the same, excepting such Parts as may in their Judgment require Secrecy; and the Yeas and Nays of the Members of either House on any question shall, at the Desire of one fifth of those Present, be entered on the Journal.

Neither House, during the Session of Congress, shall, without the Consent of the other, adjourn for more than three days, nor to any other Place than that in which the two Houses shall be sitting.

Section 6. The Senators and Representatives shall receive a Compensation for their Services, to be ascertained by Law, and paid out of the Treasury of the United States. They shall in all Cases, except Treason, Felony and Breach of the Peace, be privileged from Arrest during their Attendance at the Session of their respective Houses, and in going to and returning from the same; and for any Speech or Debate in either House, they shall not be questioned in any other Place.

No Senator or Representative shall, during the Time for which he was elected, be appointed to any civil Office under the Authority of the United States, which shall have been created, or the Emoluments whereof shall have been increased during such time; and no Person holding any Office under the United States, shall be a Member of either House during his Continuance in Office.

Section 7. All Bills for raising Revenue shall originate in the House of Representatives; but the Senate may propose or concur with Amendments as on other Bills.

Every Bill which shall have passed the House of Representatives and the Senate, shall, before it become a Law, be presented to the President of the United States: If he approve he shall sign it, but if not he shall return it, with his Objections to that House in which it shall have originated, who shall enter the Objections at large on their Journal, and proceed to reconsider it. If after such Reconsideration two thirds of that House shall agree to pass the Bill, it shall be sent, together with the Objections, to the other House, by which it shall likewise be reconsidered, and if approved by two thirds of that House, it shall become a Law. But in all such Cases the Votes of both Houses shall be determined by Yeas and Nays, and the Names of the Persons voting for and against the Bill shall be entered on the Journal of each House respectively. If any Bill shall not be returned by the President within ten Days (Sundays excepted) after it shall have been presented to him, the Same shall be a Law, in like Manner as if he had signed it, unless the Congress by their Adjournment prevent its Return, in which Case it shall not be a Law.

Every Order, Resolution, or Vote to which the Concurrence of the Senate and House of Representatives may be necessary (except on a question of Adjournment) shall be presented to the President of the United States; and before the Same shall take Effect, shall be approved by him, or being disapproved by him, shall be repassed by two thirds of the Senate and House of Representatives, according to the Rules and Limitations prescribed in the Case of a Bill.

Section 8. The Congress shall have Power To lay and collect Taxes, Duties, Imposts and Excises, to pay the Debts and provide for the common Defense and general Welfare of the United States; but all Duties, Imposts and Excises shall be uniform throughout the United States;

To borrow Money on the credit of the United States;

To regulate Commerce with foreign Nations, and among the several States, and with the Indian Tribes;

To establish an uniform Rule of Naturalization, and uniform Laws on the subject of Bankruptcies throughout the United States;

To coin Money, regulate the Value thereof, and of foreign Coin, and fix the Standard of Weights and Measures;

To provide for the Punishment of counterfeiting the Securities and current Coin of the United States;

To establish Post Offices and post Roads;

To promote the Progress of Science and useful Arts, by securing for limited Times to Authors and Inventors the exclusive Right to their respective Writings and Discoveries;

To constitute Tribunals inferior to the supreme Court;

To define and punish Piracies and Felonies committed on the high Seas, and Offences against the Law of Nations;

To declare War, grant Letters of Marque and Reprisal, and make Rules concerning Captures on Land and Water;

To raise and support Armies, but no Appropriation of Money to that Use shall be for a longer Term than two Years;

To provide and maintain a Navy;

To make Rules for the Government and Regulation of the land and naval Forces;

To provide for calling forth the Militia to execute the Laws of the Union, suppress Insurrections and repel Invasions;

To provide for organizing, arming, and disciplining the Militia, and for governing such Part of them as may be employed in the Service of the United States, reserving to the States respectively, the Appointment of the Officers, and the Authority of training the Militia according to the discipline prescribed by Congress;

To exercise exclusive Legislation in all Cases whatsoever, over such District (not exceeding ten Miles square) as may, by Cession of particular States, and the Acceptance of Congress, become the Seat of the Government of the United States, and to exercise like Authority over all Places purchased by the Consent of the Legislature of the State in which the Same shall be, for the Erection of Forts, Magazines, Arsenals, dock-Yards, and other needful Buildings;—And

To make all Laws which shall be necessary and proper for carrying into Execution the foregoing Powers, and all other Powers vested by this Constitution in the Government of the United States, or in any Department or Officer thereof.

Section 9. The Migration or Importation of such Persons as any of the States now existing shall think proper to admit, shall not be prohibited by the Congress prior to the Year one thousand eight hundred and eight, but a Tax or duty may be imposed on such Importation, not exceeding ten dollars for each Person.

The Privilege of the Writ of Habeas Corpus shall not be suspended, unless when in Cases of Rebellion or Invasion the public Safety may require it.

No Bill of Attainder or ex post facto Law shall be passed.

No Capitation or other direct, Tax shall be laid, unless in Proportion to the Census or enumeration herein before directed to be taken.[5]

No Tax or Duty shall be laid on Articles exported from any State.

No Preference shall be given by any Regulation of Commerce or Revenue to the Ports of one State over those of another; nor shall Vessels bound to, or from, one State, be obliged to enter, clear, or pay Duties in another.

No Money shall be drawn from the Treasury, but in Consequence of Appropriations made by Law; and a regular Statement and Account of the Receipts and Expenditures of all public Money shall be published from time to time.

No Title of Nobility shall be granted by the United States. And no Person holding any Office of Profit or Trust under them, shall, without the Consent of the Congress, accept of any present, Emolument, Office, or Title, of any kind whatever, from any King, Prince, or foreign State.

Section 10. No State shall enter into any Treaty, Alliance, or Confederation; grant Letters of Marque and Reprisal; coin Money; emit Bills of Credit; make any Thing but gold and silver Coin a Tender in Payment of Debts; pass any Bill of Attainder, ex post facto Law, or Law impairing the Obligation of Contracts, or grant any Title of Nobility.

No State shall, without the Consent of the Congress, lay any Imposts or Duties on Imports or Exports, except what may be absolutely necessary for executing its inspection Laws: and the net Produce of all Duties and Imposts laid by any State on Imports or Exports, shall be for the Use of the Treasury of the United States; and all such Laws shall be subject to the Revision and Control of the Congress.

No State shall, without the Consent of Congress, lay any Duty of Tonnage, keep Troops, or Ships of War in time of Peace, enter into any Agreement or Compact with another State, or with a foreign Power, or engage in War, unless actually invaded, or in such imminent Danger as will not admit of delay.

ARTICLE 2

Section 1. The executive Power shall be vested in a President of the United States of America. He shall hold his Office during the Term of four Years, and, together with the Vice President, chosen for the same Term, be elected, as follows:

Each State shall appoint, in such Manner as the Legislature thereof may direct, a Number of Electors, equal to the whole Number of Senators and Representatives to which the State may be entitled in the Congress: but no Senator or Representative, or Person holding an Office of Trust or Profit under the United States, shall be appointed an Elector.

The Electors shall meet in their respective States, and vote by Ballot for two Persons, of whom one at least shall not be an Inhabitant of the same State with themselves. And they shall make a List of all the Persons voted for, and of the Number of Votes for each; which List they shall sign and certify, and transmit sealed to the Seat of the Government of the United States, directed to the President of the Senate. The President of the Senate shall, in the Presence of the Senate and House of Representatives, open all the Certificates, and the Votes shall then be counted. The Person having the greatest Number of Votes shall be the President, if such Number be a Majority of the whole Number of Electors appointed; and if there be more than one who have such Majority, and have an equal Number of Votes, then the House of Representatives shall immediately choose by Ballot one of them for President; and if no Person have a Majority, then from the five highest on the List the said House shall in like Manner choose the President. But in choosing the President, the Votes shall be taken by States, the Representation from each State having one Vote; A quorum for this purpose shall consist of a Member or Members from two thirds of the States, and a Majority of all the States shall be necessary to a Choice. In every Case, after the Choice of the President, the Person having the greatest Number of Votes of the Electors shall be the Vice President. But if there should remain two or more who have equal Votes, the Senate shall choose from them by Ballot the Vice President.[6]

The Congress may determine the Time of choosing the Electors, and the Day on which they shall give their Votes; which Day shall be the same throughout the United States.

No Person except a natural born Citizen, or a Citizen of the United States, at the time of the Adoption of this Constitution, shall be eligible to the Office of President; neither shall any Person be eligible to that Office who shall not have attained to the Age of thirty five Years, and been fourteen Years a Resident within the United States.

In Case of the Removal of the President from Office, or of his Death, Resignation, or Inability to discharge the Powers and Duties of the said Office, the Same shall devolve on the Vice President, and the Congress may by Law provide for the Case of Removal, Death, Resignation or Inability, both of the President and Vice President, declaring what Officer shall then act as President, and such Officer shall act accordingly, until the Disability be removed, or a President shall be elected.[7]

The President shall, at stated Times, receive for his Services, a Compensation, which shall neither be increased nor diminished during the Period for which he shall have been elected, and he shall not receive within that Period any other Emolument from the United States, or any of them.

Before he enters on the Execution of his Office, he shall take the following Oath or Affirmation:—"I do solemnly swear (or affirm) that I will faithfully execute the Office of President of the United States, and will to the best of my Ability, preserve, protect and defend the Constitution of the United States."

Section 2. The President shall be Commander in Chief of the Army and Navy of the United States, and of the Militia of the several States, when called into the actual Service of the United States; he may require the Opinion, in writing, of the principal Officer in each of the executive Departments, upon any Subject relating to the Duties of their respective Offices, and he shall have Power to grant Reprieves and Pardons for Offences against the United States, except in Cases of Impeachment.

He shall have Power, by and with the Advice and Consent of the Senate, to make Treaties, provided two thirds of the Senators present concur; and he shall nominate, and by and with the Advice and Consent of the Senate, shall appoint Ambassadors, other public Ministers and Consuls, Judges of the supreme Court, and all other Officers of the United States, whose Appointments are not herein otherwise provided for, and which shall be established by Law: but the Congress may by Law vest the Appointment of such inferior Officers, as they think proper, in the President alone, in the Courts of Law, or in the Heads of Departments.

The President shall have Power to fill up all Vacancies that may happen during the Recess of the Senate, by granting Commissions which shall expire at the End of their next Session.

Section 3. He shall from time to time give to the Congress Information of the State of the Union, and recommend to their Consideration such Measures as he shall judge necessary and expedient; he may, on extraordinary Occasions, convene both Houses, or either of them, and in Case of Disagreement between them, with Respect to the Time of Adjournment, he may adjourn them to such Time as he shall think proper; he shall receive Ambassadors and other public Ministers; he shall take Care that the Laws be faithfully executed, and shall Commission all the Officers of the United States.

Section 4. The President, Vice President and all civil Officers of the United States, shall be removed from Office on Impeachment for, and Conviction of, Treason, Bribery, or other high Crimes and Misdemeanors.

ARTICLE 3

Section 1. The judicial Power of the United States shall be vested in one supreme Court, and in such inferior Courts as the Congress may from time to time ordain and establish. The Judges, both of the supreme and inferior Courts, shall hold their Offices during good Behavior, and shall, at stated Times, receive for their Services a Compensation, which shall not be diminished during their Continuance in Office.

Section 2. The judicial Power shall extend to all Cases, in Law and Equity, arising under this Constitution, the Laws of the United States, and Treaties made, or which shall be made, under their Authority;—to all Cases affecting Ambassadors, other public Ministers and Consuls;— to all Cases of admiralty and maritime Jurisdiction;—to Controversies to which the United States shall be a Party;—to Controversies between two or more States;—between a State and Citizens of another State[8];— between Citizens of different States;—between Citizens of the same State claiming Lands under Grants of different States, and between a State, or the Citizens thereof, and foreign States, Citizens or Subjects.

In all Cases affecting Ambassadors, other public Ministers and Consuls, and those in which a State shall be Party, the supreme Court shall have original Jurisdiction. In all the other Cases before mentioned, the supreme Court shall have appellate Jurisdiction, both as to Law and Fact, with such Exceptions, and under such Regulations as the Congress shall make.

The Trial of all Crimes, except in Cases of Impeachment, shall be by Jury; and such Trial shall be held in the State where the said Crimes shall have been committed; but when not committed within any State, the Trial shall be at such Place or Places as the Congress may by Law have directed.

Section 3. Treason against the United States, shall consist only in levying War against them, or in adhering to their Enemies, giving them Aid and Comfort. No Person shall be convicted of Treason unless on the Testimony of two Witnesses to the same overt Act, or on Confession in open Court.

The Congress shall have Power to declare the Punishment of Treason, but no Attainder of Treason shall work Corruption of Blood, or Forfeiture except during the Life of the Person attainted.

ARTICLE 4

Section 1. Full Faith and Credit shall be given in each State to the public Acts, Records, and judicial Proceedings of every other State.

And the Congress may by general Laws prescribe the Manner in which such Acts, Records and Proceedings shall be proved, and the Effect thereof.

Section 2. The Citizens of each State shall be entitled to all Privileges and Immunities of Citizens in the several States.

A Person charged in any State with Treason, Felony, or other Crime, who shall flee from Justice, and be found in another State, shall on Demand of the executive Authority of the State from which he fled, be delivered up, to be removed to the State having Jurisdiction of the Crime.

No Person held to Service or Labor in one State, under the Laws thereof, escaping into another, shall, in Consequence of any Law or Regulation therein, be discharged from such Service or Labor, but shall be delivered up on Claim of the Party to whom such Service or Labor may be due.[9]

Section 3. New States may be admitted by the Congress into this Union; but no new State shall be formed or erected within the Jurisdiction of any other State; nor any State be formed by the Junction of two or more States, or Parts of States, without the Consent of the Legislatures of the States concerned as well as of the Congress.

The Congress shall have Power to dispose of and make all needful Rules and Regulations respecting the Territory or other Property belonging to the United States; and nothing in this Constitution shall be so construed as to Prejudice any Claims of the United States, or of any particular State.

Section 4. The United States shall guarantee to every State in this Union a Republican Form of Government, and shall protect each of them against Invasion; and on Application of the Legislature, or of the Executive (when the Legislature cannot be convened), against domestic Violence.

ARTICLE 5

The Congress, whenever two thirds of both Houses shall deem it necessary, shall propose Amendments to this Constitution, or, on the Application of the Legislatures of two thirds of the several States, shall call a Convention for proposing Amendments, which, in either Case, shall be valid to all Intents and Purposes, as Part of this Constitution, when ratified by the Legislatures of three fourths of the several States, or by Conventions in three fourths thereof, as the one or the other Mode of Ratification may be proposed by the Congress; Provided that no Amendment which may be made prior to the Year One thousand eight hundred and eight shall in any Manner affect the first and fourth Clauses in the Ninth Section of the first Article; and that no State, without its Consent, shall be deprived of its equal Suffrage in the Senate.

ARTICLE 6

All Debts contracted and Engagements entered into, before the Adoption of this Constitution, shall be as valid against the United States under this Constitution, as under the Confederation.

This Constitution, and the Laws of the United States which shall be made in Pursuance thereof; and all Treaties made, or which shall be made, under the Authority of the United States, shall be the supreme Law of the Land; and the Judges in every State shall be bound thereby, any Thing in the Constitution or Laws of any State to the Contrary notwithstanding.

The Senators and Representatives before mentioned, and the Members of the several State Legislatures, and all executive and judicial Officers, both of the United States and of the several States, shall be bound by Oath or Affirmation, to support this Constitution; but no religious Test shall ever be required as a Qualification to any Office or public Trust under the United States.

ARTICLE 7

The Ratification of the Conventions of nine States, shall be sufficient for the Establishment of this Constitution between the States so ratifying the Same.

The Word, "the," being interlined between the seventh and eighth Lines of the first Page, the Word "Thirty" being partly written on an Erasure in the fifteenth Line of the first Page, The Words "is tried" being interlined between the thirty second and thirty third Lines of the first

Page and the Word "the" being interlined between the forty third and forty fourth Lines of the second Page.

Attest William Jackson Secretary

Done in Convention by the Unanimous Consent of the States present the Seventeenth Day of September in the Year of our Lord one thousand seven hundred and Eighty seven and of the Independence of the United States of America the Twelfth In witness whereof We have hereunto subscribed our Names,

G. Washington
    Presidt and deputy from
    Virginia

Delaware
    Geo: Read
    Gunning Bedford jun
    John Dickinson
    Richard Bassett
    Jaco: Broom

Maryland
    James McHenry
    Dan of St Thos. Jenifer
    Danl. Carroll

Virginia
    John Blair
    James Madison Jr.

North Carolina
    Wm. Blount
    Richd. Dobbs Spaight
    Hu Williamson

South Carolina
    J. Rutledge
    Charles Cotesworth Pinckney
    Charles Pinckney
    Pierce Butler

Georgia
    William Few
    Abr Baldwin

New Hampshire
    John Langdon
    Nicholas Gilman

Massachusetts
    Nathaniel Gorham
    Rufus King

Connecticut
    Wm. Saml. Johnson
    Roger Sherman

New York
    Alexander Hamilton

New Jersey
   Wil: Livingston
   David Brearley
   Wm. Paterson
   Jona: Dayton

Pennsylvania
   B Franklin
   Thomas Mifflin
   Robt. Morris
   Geo. Clymer
   Thos. FitzSimons
   Jared Ingersoll
   James Wilson
   Gouv Morris

ARTICLES OF AMENDMENT

Amendment 1

Congress shall make no law respecting an establishment of religion, or prohibiting the free exercise thereof; or abridging the freedom of speech, or of the press; or the right of the people peaceably to assemble, and to petition the Government for a redress of grievances.

Amendment 2

A well regulated Militia, being necessary to the security of a free State, the right of the people to keep and bear Arms, shall not be infringed.

Amendment 3

No Soldier shall, in time of peace be quartered in any house, without the consent of the Owner, nor in time of war, but in a manner to be prescribed by law.

Amendment 4

The right of the people to be secure in their persons, houses, papers, and effects, against unreasonable searches and seizures, shall not be violated, and no Warrants shall issue, but upon probable cause, supported by Oath or affirmation, and particularly describing the place to be searched, and the persons or things to be seized.

Amendment 5

No person shall be held to answer for a capital, or otherwise infamous crime, unless on a presentment or indictment of a Grand Jury, except in cases arising in the land or naval forces, or in the Militia, when in actual service in time of War or public danger; nor shall any person be subject for the same offense to be twice put in jeopardy of life or limb; nor shall be compelled in any criminal case to be a witness against himself, nor be deprived of life, liberty, or property, without due process of law; nor shall private property be taken for public use, without just compensation.

Amendment 6

In all criminal prosecutions, the accused shall enjoy the right to a speedy and public trial, by an impartial jury of the State and district wherein the crime shall have been committed, which district shall have been previously ascertained by law, and to be informed of the nature and cause of the accusation; to be confronted with the witnesses against him; to have compulsory process for obtaining witnesses in his favor, and to have the Assistance of Counsel for his defense.

Amendment 7

In Suits at common law, where the value in controversy shall exceed twenty dollars, the right of trial by jury shall be preserved, and no fact tried by a jury, shall be otherwise re-examined in any Court of the United States, than according to the rules of the common law.

Amendment 8

Excessive bail shall not be required, nor excessive fines imposed, nor cruel and unusual punishments inflicted.

Amendment 9

The enumeration in the Constitution, of certain rights, shall not be construed to deny or disparage others retained by the people.

Amendment 10

The powers not delegated to the United States by the Constitution, nor prohibited by it to the States, are reserved to the States respectively, or to the people.

Amendment 11

The Judicial power of the United States shall not be construed to extend to any suit in law or equity, commenced or prosecuted against one of the United States by Citizens of another State, or by Citizens or Subjects of any Foreign State.

Amendment 12

The Electors shall meet in their respective states and vote by ballot for President and Vice-President, one of whom, at least, shall not be an inhabitant of the same state with themselves; they shall name in their ballots the person voted for as President, and in distinct ballots the person voted for as Vice-President, and they shall make distinct lists of all persons voted for as President, and of all persons voted for as Vice-President, and of the number of votes for each, which lists they shall sign and certify, and transmit sealed to the seat of the government of the United States, directed to the President of the Senate;—the President of the Senate shall, in the presence of the Senate and House of Representatives, open all the certificates and the votes shall then be counted;—The person having the greatest number of votes for President, shall be the President, if such number be a majority of the whole number of Electors appointed; and if no person have such majority, then from the persons having the highest numbers not exceeding three on the list of those voted for as President, the House of Representatives shall choose immediately, by ballot, the President. But in choosing the President, the votes shall be taken by states, the representation from each state having one vote; a quorum for this purpose shall consist of a member or members from two-thirds of the states, and a majority of all the states shall be necessary to a choice. And if the House of Representatives shall not choose a President whenever the right of choice shall devolve upon them, before the fourth day of March next following, then the Vice-President shall act as President, as in case of the death or other constitutional disability of the President.—[10] The person having the greatest number of votes as Vice-President, shall be the Vice-President, if such number be a majority of the whole number of Electors appointed, and if no person have a majority, then from the two highest numbers on the list, the Senate shall choose the Vice-President; a quorum for the purpose shall consist of two-thirds of the whole number of Senators, and a majority of the whole number shall be necessary to a choice. But no person constitutionally ineligible to the office of President shall be eligible to that of Vice-President of the United States.

Amendment 13

Section 1. Neither slavery nor involuntary servitude, except as a punishment for crime whereof the party shall have been duly convicted, shall exist within the United States, or any place subject to their jurisdiction.

Section 2. Congress shall have power to enforce this article by appropriate legislation.

Amendment 14

Section 1. All persons born or naturalized in the United States, and subject to the jurisdiction thereof, are citizens of the United States and of the State wherein they reside. No State shall make or enforce any law which shall abridge the privileges or immunities of citizens of the United States; nor shall any State deprive any person of life, liberty, or property, without due process of law; nor deny to any person within its jurisdiction the equal protection of the laws.

Section 2. Representatives shall be apportioned among the several States according to their respective numbers, counting the whole number of persons in each State, excluding Indians not taxed. But when the right to vote at any election for the choice of electors for President and Vice-President of the United States, Representatives in Congress, the Executive and Judicial officers of a State, or the members of the Legislature thereof, is denied to any of the male inhabitants of such State, being twenty-one years of age,[11] and citizens of the United States, or in any way abridged, except for participation in rebellion, or other crime, the basis of representation therein shall be reduced in the proportion which the number of such male citizens shall bear to the whole number of male citizens twenty-one years of age in such State.

Section 3. No person shall be a Senator or Representative in Congress, or elector of President and Vice-President, or hold any office, civil or military, under the United States, or under any State, who, having previously taken an oath, as a member of Congress, or as an officer of the United States, or as a member of any State legislature, or as an executive or judicial officer of any State, to support the Constitution of the United States, shall have engaged in insurrection or rebellion against the same, or given aid or comfort to the enemies thereof. But Congress may by a vote of two-thirds of each House, remove such disability.

Section 4. The validity of the public debt of the United States, authorized by law, including debts incurred for payment of pensions and bounties for services in suppressing insurrection or rebellion, shall not be questioned. But neither the United States nor any State shall assume or pay any debt or obligation incurred in aid of insurrection or rebellion against the United States, or any claim for the loss or eman- cipation of any slave; but all such debts, obligations and claims shall be held illegal and void.

Section 5. The Congress shall have the power to enforce, by appropriate legislation, the provisions of this article.

Amendment 15

Section 1. The right of citizens of the United States to vote shall not be denied or abridged by the United States or by any State on account of race, color, or previous condition of servitude—

Section 2. The Congress shall have the power to enforce this article by appropriate legislation.

Amendment 16

The Congress shall have power to lay and collect taxes on incomes, from whatever source derived, without apportionment among the several States, and without regard to any census or enumeration.

Amendment 17

The Senate of the United States shall be composed of two Senators from each State, elected by the people thereof, for six years; and each Senator shall have one vote. The electors in each State shall have the qualifications requisite for electors of the most numerous branch of the State legislatures.

When vacancies happen in the representation of any State in the Senate, the executive authority of such State shall issue writs of election to fill such vacancies: Provided, That the legislature of any State may empower the executive thereof to make temporary appointments until the people fill the vacancies by election as the legislature may direct.

This amendment shall not be so construed as to affect the election or term of any Senator chosen before it becomes valid as part of the Constitution.

Amendment 18

Section 1. After one year from the ratification of this article the manufacture, sale, or transportation of intoxicating liquors within, the importation thereof into, or the exportation thereof from the United States and all territory subject to the jurisdiction thereof for beverage purposes is hereby prohibited.

Section 2. The Congress and the several States shall have concurrent power to enforce this article by appropriate legislation.

Section 3. This article shall be inoperative unless it shall have been ratified as an amendment to the Constitution by the legislatures of the several States, as provided in the Constitution, within seven years from the date of the submission hereof to the States by the Congress.[12]

Amendment 19

The right of citizens of the United States to vote shall not be denied or abridged by the United States or by any State on account of sex.

Congress shall have power to enforce this article by appropriate legislation.

Amendment 20

Section 1. The terms of the President and the Vice President shall end at noon on the 20th day of January, and the terms of Senators and Representatives at noon on the 3d day of January, of the years in which such terms would have ended if this article had not been ratified; and the terms of their successors shall then begin.

Section 2. The Congress shall assemble at least once in every year, and such meeting shall begin at noon on the 3d day of January, unless they shall by law appoint a different day.

Section 3. If, at the time fixed for the beginning of the term of the President, the President elect shall have died, the Vice President elect shall become President. If a President shall not have been chosen before the time fixed for the beginning of his term, or if the President elect shall have failed to qualify, then the Vice President elect shall act as President until a President shall have qualified; and the Congress may by law provide for the case wherein neither a President elect nor a Vice President shall have qualified, declaring who shall then act as President, or the manner in which one who is to act shall be selected, and such person shall act accordingly until a President or Vice President shall have qualified.

Section 4. The Congress may by law provide for the case of the death of any of the persons from whom the House of Representatives may choose a President whenever the right of choice shall have devolved upon them, and for the case of the death of any of the persons from whom the Senate may choose a Vice President whenever the right of choice shall have devolved upon them.

Section 5. Sections 1 and 2 shall take effect on the 15th day of October following the ratification of this article.

Section 6. This article shall be inoperative unless it shall have been ratified as an amendment to the Constitution by the legislatures of three-fourths of the several States within seven years from the date of its submission.

Amendment 21

Section 1. The eighteenth article of amendment to the Constitution of the United States is hereby repealed.

Section 2. The transportation or importation into any State, Territory, or Possession of the United States for delivery or use therein of intoxicating liquors, in violation of the laws thereof, is hereby prohibited.

Section 3. This article shall be inoperative unless it shall have been ratified as an amendment to the Constitution by conventions in the several States, as provided in the Constitution, within seven years from the date of the submission hereof to the States by the Congress.

Amendment 22

Section 1. No person shall be elected to the office of the President more than twice, and no person who has held the office of President, or acted as President, for more than two years of a term to which some other person was elected President shall be elected to the office of President more than once. But this Article shall not apply to any person holding the office of President when this Article was proposed by Congress, and shall not prevent any person who may be holding the office of President, or acting as President, during the term within which this Article becomes operative from holding the office of President or acting as President during the remainder of such term.

Section 2. This article shall be inoperative unless it shall have been ratified as an amendment to the Constitution by the legislatures of three-fourths of the several States within seven years from the date of its submission to the States by the Congress.

Amendment 23

Section 1. The District constituting the seat of Government of the United States shall appoint in such manner as Congress may direct:

A number of electors of President and Vice President equal to the whole number of Senators and Representatives in Congress to which the District would be entitled if it were a State, but in no event more than the least populous State; they shall be in addition to those appointed by the States, but they shall be considered, for the purposes of the election of President and Vice President, to be electors appointed by a State; and they shall meet in the District and perform such duties as provided by the twelfth article of amendment.

Section 2. The Congress shall have power to enforce this article by appropriate legislation.

Amendment 24

Section 1. The right of citizens of the United States to vote in any primary or other election for President or Vice President, for electors for President or Vice President, or for Senator or Representative in Congress, shall not be denied or abridged by the United States or any State by reason of failure to pay poll tax or other tax.

Section 2. The Congress shall have power to enforce this article by appropriate legislation.

Amendment 25

Section 1. In case of the removal of the President from office or of his death or resignation, the Vice President shall become President.

Section 2. Whenever there is a vacancy in the office of the Vice President, the President shall nominate a Vice President who shall take office upon confirmation by a majority vote of both Houses of Congress.

Section 3. Whenever the President transmits to the President pro tempore of the Senate and the Speaker of the House of Representatives his written declaration that he is unable to discharge the powers and duties of his office, and until he transmits to them a written declaration to the contrary, such powers and duties shall be discharged by the Vice President as Acting President.

Section 4. Whenever the Vice President and a majority of either the principal officers of the executive departments or of such other body as Congress may by law provide, transmit to the President pro tempore of the Senate and the Speaker of the House of Representatives their written declaration that the President is unable to discharge the powers and duties of his office, the Vice President shall immediately assume the powers and duties of the office as Acting President.

Thereafter, when the President transmits to the President pro tempore of the Senate and the Speaker of the House of Representatives his written declaration that no inability exists, he shall resume the powers and duties of his office unless the Vice President and a majority of either the principal officers of the executive department or of such other body as Congress may by law provide, transmit within four days to the President pro tempore of the Senate and the Speaker of the House of Representatives their written declaration that the President is unable to discharge the powers and duties of his office. Thereupon Congress shall decide the issue, assembling within forty-eight hours for that purpose if not in session. If the Congress, within twenty-one days after receipt of the latter written declaration, or, if Congress is not in session, within twenty-one days after Congress is required to assemble, determines by two-thirds vote of both Houses that the President is unable to discharge the powers and duties of his office, the Vice President shall continue to discharge the same as Acting President; otherwise, the President shall resume the powers and duties of his office.

Amendment 26

Section 1. The right of citizens of the United States, who are eighteen years of age or older, to vote shall not be denied or abridged by the United States or by any State on account of age.

Section 2. The Congress shall have power to enforce this article by appropriate legislation.

Amendment 27

No law, varying the compensation for the services of the Senators and Representatives, shall take effect, until an election of representatives shall have intervened.

NOTES

1. Modified by the Fourteenth Amendment.
2. Modified by the Seventeenth Amendment.
3. Also modified by the Seventeenth Amendment.
4. Modified by the Twentieth Amendment; part of the Twelfth Amendment was also superseded by the Twentieth.
5. Modified by the Sixteenth Amendment.
6. Partially superseded by the Twelfth Amendment.
7. Affected by the Twenty-fifth Amendment.
8. Modified by the Eleventh Amendment.
9. Superseded by the Thirteenth Amendment.
10. Superseded by the Twentieth Amendment.
11. Modified by the Twenty-sixth Amendment.
12. The Eighteenth Amendment was repealed by the Twenty-first.

ACKNOWLEDGMENTS

The task of writing a book which attempts to distill your political and legal philosophy is not an easy one. This is my first work of book length. I would not have been able to assemble the ideas and to articulate the philosophy in this book were it not for many who helped to mold my thinking and frame my ideas throughout my life.

My parents, Andrew and Rita, of course, taught me all the truths I know. They and my brothers Jim and Larry always pressed me to defend my novel ideas at the dinner table.

When I was an undergraduate at Princeton University, I was privileged to have the brilliant and charming Walter Murphy teach me his popular course, Constitutional Interpretation. Professor Murphy was then the McCormick Professor of Jurisprudence, one of the most sought after chairs in legal academia, a seat that was once held by a young Princeton professor named Woodrow Wilson. Professor Murphy opened my eyes to the power of the judiciary to influence our culture for good and evil.

When I was a law student at the University of Notre Dame Law School, I was taught by many very bright minds. Foremost among them was Professor Charles E. Rice. Professor Rice, a fierce Roman Catholic and a staunch defender of the Constitution, instilled in me the values of individual liberty, limited government, and patience.

My best buddies in college and law school, Dan Cheely, Harding Jones, John Roland, Frank Elliot, Tim Westman, Dave Condit, Jerry

Raymond, Steve Glauberman, Frank Marasco, and I endlessly debated all these ideas.

Since practicing law, and sitting on the bench, I have, as well, been influenced by many great minds. Among them is the late Judge J. Daniel Mahoney, of the United States Court of Appeals for the Second Circuit, the late Justice Morris Pashman, of the Supreme Court of New Jersey, the wonderful Judge Dickenson R. Debevoise, of the United States District Court for the District of New Jersey, the unflinching Howard A. Glickstein, Dean Emeritus of Touro Law School, and the brilliant Judge Alexander P. Waugh Jr., of the Superior Court of New Jersey.

My work in putting this book together could not have occurred, but for the assistance of my dogged research assistant, Aaron Schechter, who at this writing is one of the brightest young members of the third-year class at New York University Law School; the help of my long-time assistant, Cheryl Romeo, who encouraged me to write this book; the energy of my personal assistant at Fox, Ciara Sullivan, who tolerates my endless and incessant revisions with cheerfulness; and the patience of James Conley Sheil, who read the drafts of this book and who challenged all of my thoughts and ideas and caused me to defend or to reassess them.

And, of course, I would not have an audience for this book were at not for Roger Ailes, founder, Chairman, and Chief Executive Officer of Fox News Channel. Mr. Ailes has the most brilliant mind in television and has its best sense of humor, and he gave this former New Jersey judge a chance, and a lot of second chances, at talking to a camera.

Whatever faults this work has are mine. Any good it may cause, and any government reform it may bring about, is because of those who helped me.

INDEX